FOUNDATION ATLAS

SUBJECT LIST	UK Map Section	World Map Section
Acid rain	17, 24	
Age/sex pyramids	22	
Agriculture	18, 24	
Aerial photography	6, 7	
Barley	18	
Climate graphs	16	30
Coal	19	39
Defence	23	
Deforestation		32
Desertification		32
Earthquakes		33
Employment	20, 23	37
Energy production and consumption	19	39
Family size		35
Fishing	18	
Food intake		37
Fuels		39
Illiteracy		36
Industrial accidents		32
Land use	18, 24	38
Life expectancy		35
Manufacturing	20	
Minerals		38
Motorways	21	
National parks	21	
Natural gas	19	39
Natural vegetation	24	32
Oil	19	39
Pollution	24	32
Population change	22, 23	34
Population density	22, 23	34
Population per doctor		37
Ports	20	
Railways	21	
Rainfall	16, 24	31
Satellite imagery	8, 9	
Services	20, 23	
Sunshine hours	16	
Temperature	16, 24	31
Tourism	21	
Unemployment	20	
Urban population		34
Volcanoes		33
Water supply	17	36
Wealth	23	
Weather map	16	
Wheat	18	
Young and old	22	

Published by Heinemann Educational,
a division of Reed Educational and Professional Publishing Ltd,
Halley Court, Jordan Hill, Oxford OX2 8EJ

OXFORD MADRID ATHENS FLORENCE PRAGUE CHICAGO
PORTSMOUTH NH (USA) MEXICO CITY SÃO PAULO SINGAPORE
KUALA LUMPUR TOKYO MELBOURNE AUCKLAND NAIROBI
KAMPALA IBADAN GABORONE JOHANNESBURG

in association with George Philip Ltd,
Michelin House, 81 Fulham Road, London SW3 6RB

Copyright © 1997 Reed International Books Ltd
Cartography by Philip's
First published 1989
This edition published 1997

A catalogue record for this book is available from the British Library
ISBN 0-435-35009-9 (paper)
         0-435-35008-0 (cased)
Printed and bound in China

Below is a slice through the map of England and Wales on page 10. It is used here to explain the meaning of the lines, colours and symbols.

Sea
Coastline
Colours showing the height of the land.
River
River name
National boundary (international boundaries are shown as ——)
Lake
Line of latitude
Line of longitude
Highest point, with height in metres
County boundary
Main railway
Main road
Motorway
Motorway number
Canal
Airport
Symbols locating towns. The larger the population of the town, the larger the symbol.

HEIGHT OF LAND

There is an explanation like the one on the right on every page where different colours are used to show the height of the land above sea level. There is also a colour for land below sea level.

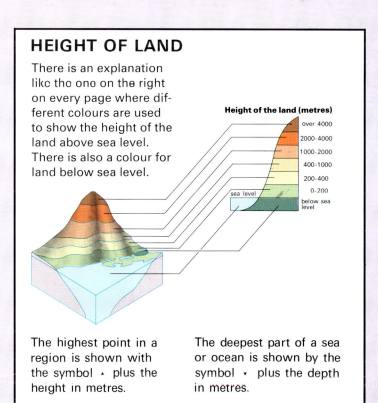

The highest point in a region is shown with the symbol ▲ plus the height in metres.

The deepest part of a sea or ocean is shown by the symbol ▾ plus the depth in metres.

SCALE BAR

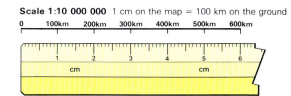

Every map has a scale statement, scale bar and ruler with it. For a full explanation of scale and how to use the scale bar, see page 2.

SCALE COMPARISON MAP

This map, or one of England and Wales appears on the maps of the continents at the same scale as the main map. They give an idea of size.

LOCATOR MAP

There is a small map such as this on every map page. The red area shows how the main map fits into its larger region.

Acknowledgements
page 6 photograph © Patricia & Angus Macdonald
page 7 map extract © Crown Copyright
page 7 photograph © Crown Copyright
pages 8 and 9 photographs © NRSC

Types of Scale

In this atlas the scale of the map is shown in three ways:-

1. **A written statement** - this tells you how many kilometres on the Earth are represented by one centimetre on the map.

1cm on the map = 20km on the ground

2. **Ratio** - this tells you that one on the map represents two million of the same unit on the ground.

1:2 000 000

3. **Scale** - this shows you the scale as a line or bar with a section of ruler beneath it.

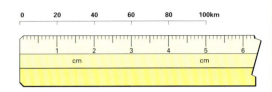

How to measure distance

The map on the right is a small part of the map of Southern Europe which is on page 6 in the World Map section of the atlas.

The scale of the map extract is shown below:

Scale 1:10 000 000   1cm on the map = 100km on the ground

To measure the distance from London to Paris you can use any of the three methods described above.

For example:-

Using the written statement

Using the scale above you can see that 1cm on the map represents 100km on the ground.

Measure the distance on the map between London and Paris. You will see that this is about 3.5cm.

If 1cm = 100km

then 3.5cm = 350km   (3.5 x 100)

Using the Ratio

Using the scale above you can see that the ratio is 1:10 000 000

We know that the distance on the map between the cities is 3.5cm and we know from the ratio that 1cm on the map = 10 000 000cm on the ground. We multiply the map distance by the ratio.

= 3.5 x 10 000 000cm
= 35 000 000cm
= 350 000m
= **350km**

Using the Scale

We know that the distance on the map between the cities is 3.5cm.

Using the scale, measure 3.5cm along this (or use the yellow section of ruler as a guide) and read off the distance.

Using these 3 methods now work out the distance between London and Birmingham on the map above. Your teacher could tell you if your answer is correct.

The map on the left is an extract from the map of Asia on page 10 in the World Map section of the atlas. Below, you can see the scale of this map. Calculate the distance between Calcutta and Bangkok.

Scale 1:45 000 000   1cm on the map = 450km on the ground

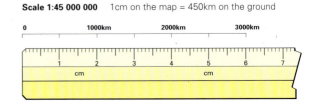

Different Sizes of Scale

The table on the right shows the distances between London - Paris and Bangkok - Calcutta. The map distances are both 3.5cm but the actual distances are very different. This is because the maps are at different scales.

	Map Distance	Scale	Actual Distance
London - Paris	3.5cm	1:10 000 000	350km
Bangkok - Calcutta	3.5cm	1:45 000 000	1 575km

On the continent maps, in the World Map section of this atlas, are Scale Comparison maps. These show you the size of the British Isles drawn at the same scale as the main map on that page. This is to give you an idea of the size of that continent.

Below are three maps which appear in this atlas.

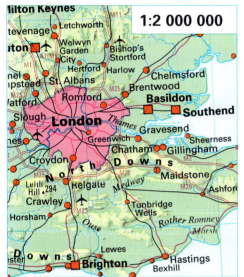

The maps all show London, but the map above shows much more detail than the maps on the right. The map above is a larger scale map than the maps on the right.

Large Scale means a **large** map of a **small** area

Small Scale means a **small** map of a **large** area

Notice how the ratios are getting larger as the scale of the map gets smaller.

Direction on the Maps

On most of the atlas maps, North is at the top of the page. Longitude lines run from South to North. These usually curve a little because the Earth is a globe and not a flat shape.

Points of the Compass

Below is a drawing of the points of the compass. North, East, South and West are called **cardinal points**. Direction is sometimes given in degrees. This is measured going clockwise from North. To help you remember the order of the compass points try to learn this sentence:
  Naughty **E**lephants **S**quirt **W**ater

Using a Compass

Compasses have a needle with a magnetic tip. The tip is attracted towards the Magnetic North Pole which is close to the North Pole. The compass tells you where North is. You can see the Magnetic North Pole on the diagram below.

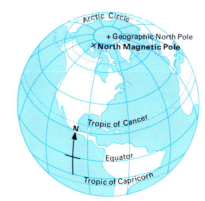

THE MAGNETIC NORTH POLE

Activities

Look at the map below.
If Keswick is South of Edinburgh then.
• Armagh is _____ - _____ of Oxford.
• Fort William is _____ of Edinburgh.
• Ilfracombe is _____ of Oxford.
Look at the map on pages 10-11 of the British Isles section.
• Which is the most Southerly town shown in England ?
• Which is the most Westerly town shown in Wales ?

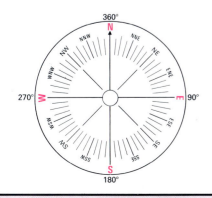

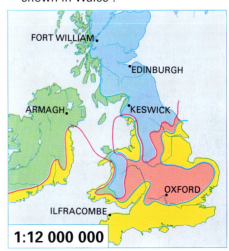

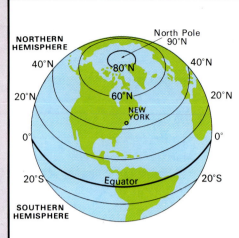

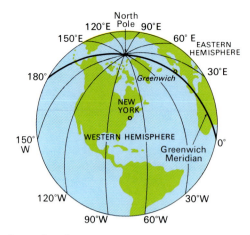

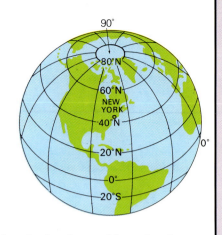

Latitude

Lines of latitude cross the atlas maps from East to West. The Equator is at 0. All other lines of latitude are either North of the Equator, or South of the Equator. Line 40°N is almost half way towards the North Pole. The North Pole is at 90°N.

At the Equator a degree measures about 110km.

Longitude

Lines of longitude run from North to South. These lines meet at the North Pole and the South Pole. Longitude 0 passes through Greenwich. This line is also called the Greenwich Meridian. Lines of longitude are either East of 0 or West of 0. There are 180 degrees of longitude both East and West of 0.

Using latitude and longitude

Latitude and longitude lines make a grid. You can find a place if you know its latitude and longitude number. The latitude number is either North or South of the Equator. The longitude number is either East or West of the Greenwich Meridian.

Special latitude lines

Some special latitude lines are shown on maps. The diagrams in the World Map section on page 40 show that the sun is only overhead vertically in the tropical regions. These regions are between 23°30' North and South of the Equator. On maps these are shown as blue dotted lines. The **Tropic of Cancer** is at 23°30'N and the **Tropic of Capricorn** is at 23°30'S.

In the North and South Polar regions there are places where the Sun does not rise or set above the horizon at certain times of the year. These places are also shown by a blue dotted line. The **Arctic Circle** is at 66°30'N and the **Antarctic Circle** is at 66°30'S.

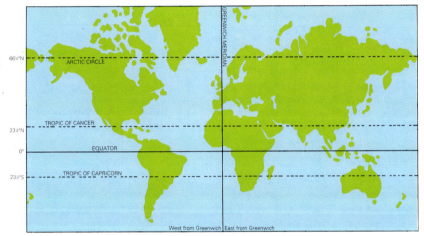

Latitude and longitude in this atlas

In this atlas lines of latitude and longitude are blue.

On large scale maps such as those in the British Isles section, pages 10 – 13, there is a line for every degree. On smaller scale maps only every other, every fifth or even tenth line is shown.

The map on the right shows the British Isles. The latitude and longitude lines are numbered at the edges of the map. The bottom of the map shows whether a place is East or West of Greenwich. The side of the map tells you how far North from the Equator the line is.

Around the edges of the map are small yellow pointers with letters and numbers in. Columns made by longitude lines have letters, rows made by latitude lines have numbers.

In the index at the end of the atlas places have number-letter references as well as latitude and longitude numbers.

On the map opposite, London is in rectangle **8M** (this is where row 8 crosses with column M). Edinburgh is in **4J** and Dublin is in **6F**.

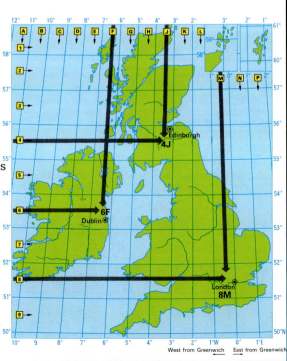

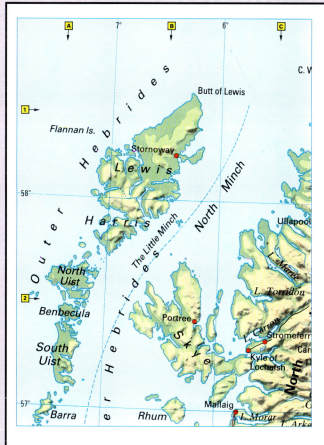

How to find a place

The map on the left is an extract from the map of Scotland on page 12 of the British Isles section. If you want to find Stornoway in the atlas you must look in the British Isles index. Places are listed alphabetically. You will find the following entry:

Stornoway............**12 1B** 58°N 6°W

The number in bold type is the page number where the map appears. The figure and letter which follow the page number give the grid rectangle on the map in which the feature appears. Here we can see that Stornoway is on page 12 in the rectangle where row 1 crosses column B.

The latitude and longitude number corresponds with the numbered lines on the map. The first set of figures represent the latitude and the second set represent the longitude. The unit of measurement for latitude and longitude is the degree (°) which is divided into minutes ('). Here, only full degrees are given.

Latitude and longitude can be used to locate places more accurately on smaller scale maps such as those in the World Map section.

All rivers are indexed to their mouth or confluence and in the index they are followed by the symbol ⇢.

Making Maps

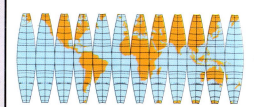

One of the greatest problems in making maps is how to draw the curved surface of the globe on a flat piece of paper. The map above shows one way of putting the globe onto paper, but because it splits up the land and sea it is not very useful.

The map above is better. It is a good map because it shows the correct size of places. It is an **equal area** map. For example, Australia is the correct size in relation to North America and Europe is the correct size in relation to Africa.

Comparing areas is a useful way of checking the accuracy of maps. Comparing Greenland (2.2 million km²) with Australia (7.7 million km²) is a good 'area test'.

A better shape at the edges of the map can be made by splitting the map (above).

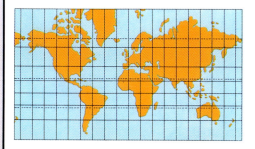

The map on the left is called **Mercator**. It has been used since the 16th century. The area scale is not equal area. All sea and air maps are drawn on this type of map.

The scale of distances is difficult to put on a map. On the above map the Equator and Greenwich Meridian are true to scale.

On the Mercator map, scale is correct along the Equator but is less correct towards the Poles.

In this atlas most maps are reasonable for area and scale. Latitude lines are curves and longitude lines are straight lines or curves.

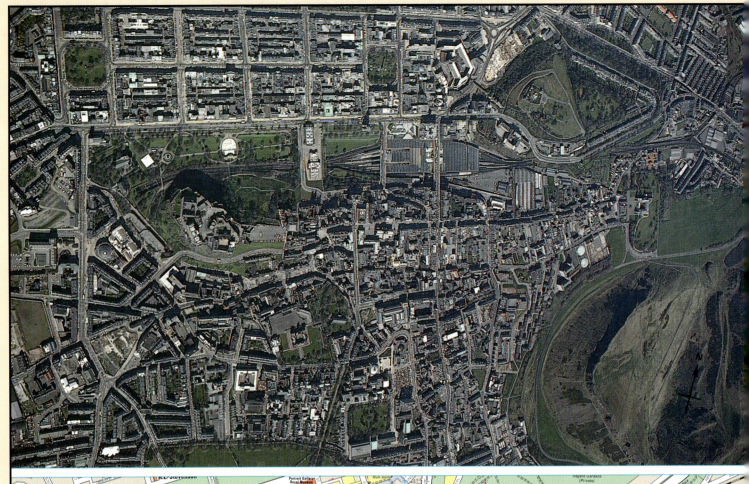

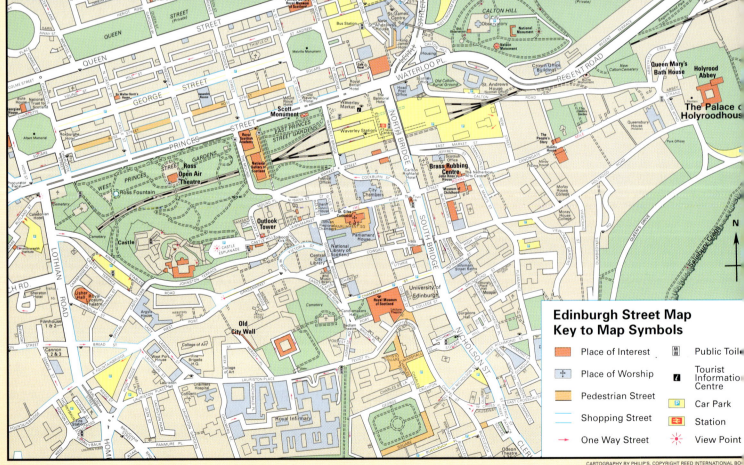

**Edinburgh Street Map
Key to Map Symbols**

Place of Interest

Place of Worship

Pedestrian Street

Shopping Street

One Way Street

Public Toilet

Tourist Information Centre

Car Park

Station

View Point

CARTOGRAPHY BY PHILIP'S. COPYRIGHT REED INTERNATIONAL BO

Edinburgh

Scale 1:10 000   1 cm on the map and aerial photograph = 100 metres on the ground

0   500 metres   1 km

cm   cm

O.S. Pathfinder Map of St. Ives

Key to Map Symbols

Roads and Paths

- A 31(T) — Trunk or main road
- B 3074 — Secondary road
- Road more than 4 metres wide
- Road less than 4 metres wide
- Other road, drive or track
- Path
- Public right of way

Railways

- Single track
- Cutting, embankment

Symbols

- Place of worship
- Building, important building
- Lighthouse, beacon
- Triangulation pillar
- W, Spr — Well, spring
- Cliff
- Water, sand and shingle

Vegetation

- Coniferous forest
- Non-coniferous forest
- Coppice
- Orchard
- Scrub
- Bracken, rough grassland

Heights

- ˙116 — Spot heights in metres
- Contours are in 5 metre intervals

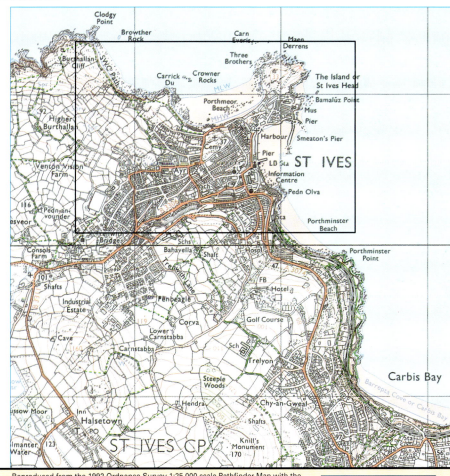

Reproduced from the 1992 Ordnance Survey 1:25,000 scale Pathfinder Map with the permission of the Controller of Her Majesty's Stationery Office © Crown Copyright

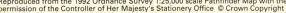

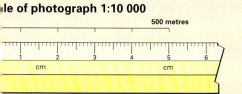

le of photograph 1:10 000

500 metres

on the photograph = 100 metres on the ground

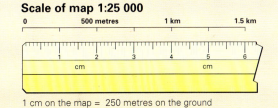

Scale of map 1:25 000

0   500 metres   1 km   1.5 km

1 cm on the map = 250 metres on the ground

St. Ives

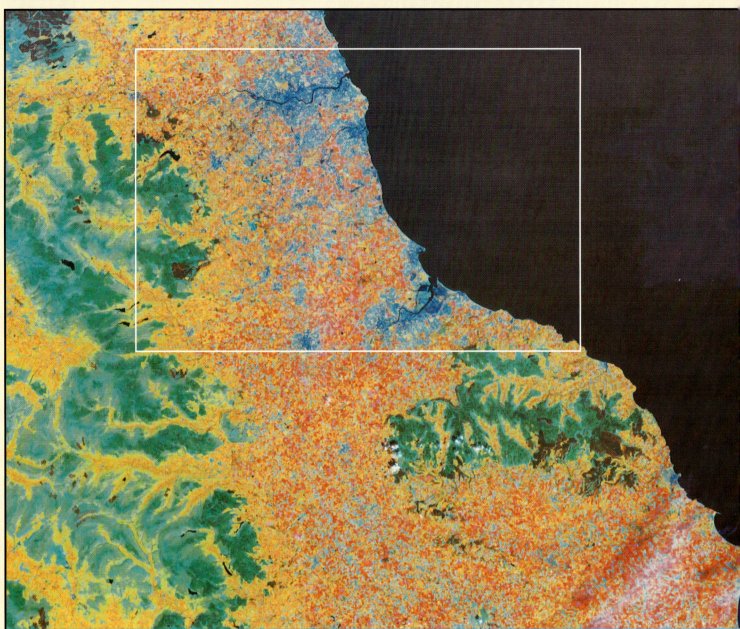

British Isles from Space

The images on pages 8 and 9 are produced from data captured by NASA's Landsat spacecraft. It travels around the Earth at a height of over 900 kilometres. It scans every part of the Earth's surface once every 18 days. The data is transmitted back to Earth where it is printed in false colours to make certain features stand out. On these pages arable land appears red, pasture orange, woodland dark brown, water dark blue and built up areas grey-blue. The image on page 8 shows North-East England in summer. The image on page 9 shows North Wales in winter. Comparing the maps with the images helps to identify specific features on the images.

Scale 1:760 000   1 cm on the map and satellite image = 7.6 km on the ground

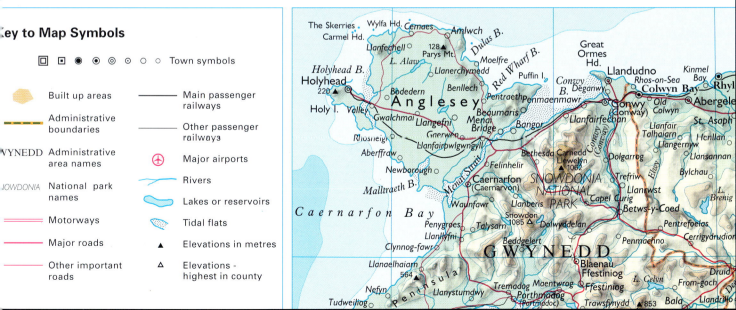

Key to Map Symbols

□ ▣ ● ◉ ◎ ○ ○ Town symbols

Built up areas

Administrative boundaries

GWYNEDD Administrative area names

SNOWDONIA National park names

Motorways

Major roads

Other important roads

Main passenger railways

Other passenger railways

⊕ Major airports

Rivers

Lakes or reservoirs

Tidal flats

▲ Elevations in metres

△ Elevations – highest in county

The Skerries
Carmel Hd. Wylfa Hd. Cemaes Amlwch
Llanfechell Dulas B.
Holyhead B. L. Alaw Parys Mt. 128▲ Moelfre
Holyhead Llanerchymedd Red Wharf B. Puffin I.
220▲ Bodedern Benllech Pentraeth Penmaenmawr
Holy I. Valley **Anglesey** Beaumaris Great Ormes Hd.
Gwalchmai Llangefni Menai Bangor Llandudno Rhos-on-Sea Kinmel Bay
Rhosneigr Bridge Conwy Deganwy Colwyn Bay Rhyl
Aberffraw Llanfairpwllgwyngyll B. Conwy Old Abergele
Newborough Felinheli (Conway) Colwyn St. Asaph
Malltraeth B. Caernarfon Bethesda Carnedd Llanfair Hen Ilan
Caernarfon Bay (Caernarvon) SNOWDONIA Llewelyn Trefriw Llanrwst Talhaiarn Llangernyw
Waunfawr 1062▲ NATIONAL Dolgarrog Llansannan Bylchau
Penygroes Llanberis PARK Capel Curig L. Brenig
Llanllyfni Talysarn Snowdon Betws-y-Coed Pentrefoelas
Clynnog-fawr 1085▲ Dolwyddelan Penmachno Cerrigydrudion
Llanaelhaiarn **GWYNEDD** Blaenau Druid
564△ Ffestiniog L. Celyn From-goch
Nefyn Tremadog Maentwrog Ffestiniog Bala Llandrillo
Peninsula Llanystumdwy Porthmadog Trawsfynydd 853▲
Tudweiliog (Portmadoc)

RAPHY BY PHILIP'S. COPYRIGHT REED INTERNATIONAL BOOKS LTD

Scale 1:760 000   1 cm on the map and satellite image = 7.6 km on the ground

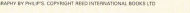

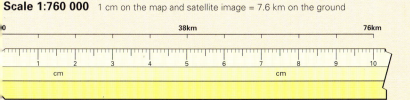

0 38km 76km

cm   cm

Scale 1:2 000 000

150 km
100 km
50 km
0

N O R T H   S E A

I R I S H   S E A

North Channel

The Wash

Firth of Forth
Firth of Clyde
Solway Firth
Morecambe Bay
Caernarfon Bay
Conwy Bay

S C O T L A N D
Southern Uplands
NORTHERN IRELAND
WALES

Pennines
Cheviot Hills
Lake District
Cumbrian Mts.
N. York Moors
Yorkshire Wolds
Lincolnshire Wolds
Holderness
Wensleydale
Wharfedale
The Peak

Scafell Pike 978
Cross Fell 893
The Cheviot 816
Snowdon 1085
Cader Idris
Shaefell 620
Merrick 843
Ben Lomond
Broad Law 840
Boat Fell 874
Helvellyn 950

Edinburgh, Dunfermline, Kinross, Kirkcaldy, Glenrothes, Stirling, Falkirk, Livingston, Peebles, Lanark, Coatbridge, Airdrie, Glasgow, Motherwell, Cumbernauld, Paisley, Hamilton, East Kilbride, Greenock, Dumbarton, Rothesay, Largs, Johnstone, Irvine, Kilmarnock, Cumnock, Ayr, Newton Stewart, Wigtown, Stranraer

Inverara, Lochgilphead, L. Awe, Arran, Campbeltown, Mull of Kintyre, Girvan, Ballantrae

Berwick-upon-Tweed, St. Abb's Head, Eyemouth, Dunbar, Coldstream, Kelso, Jedburgh, Galashiels, Hawick, Lockerbie, Gretna Green, Annan, Dumfries, Carlisle, Penrith, Kendal, Appleby, Barnard Castle, Bishop Auckland, Consett, Durham, Darlington, Northallerton, Richmond, Ripon, Skipton, Harrogate, Keighley, Nelson, Burnley, Accrington, Blackburn

Newcastle-upon-Tyne, Gateshead, Washington, South Shields, Tynemouth, Sunderland, Houghton-le-Spring, Hartlepool, Redcar, Billingham, Middlesbrough, Stockton, Blyth, Morpeth, Alnwick, Rothbury

Whitby, Scarborough, Bridlington, Flamborough Hd., Filey, Driffield, Hull, Kingston upon Hull, Withernsea, Spurn Head, Cleethorpes, Grimsby, Immingham, Scunthorpe, Goole, Selby, York, Malton, Pickering, Doncaster, Rotherham, Sheffield, Barnsley, Wakefield, Leeds, Bradford, Halifax, Huddersfield, Castleford, Pontefract

Manchester, Stockport, Warrington, Runcorn, Salford, Bolton, Bury, Rochdale, Oldham, Ashton-under-Lyne, Sale, Wigan, St. Helens, Widnes, Chester, Crewe, Congleton, Macclesfield, Buxton, Matlock, Chesterfield, Mansfield, Worksop, Newark, Lincoln, Gainsborough, Brigg, Boston, Spalding, Grantham, Sutton in Ashfield, Long Eaton, Loughborough, Nottingham, Ilkeston, Derby, Burton upon Trent, Stafford, Stoke on Trent, Newcastle-under-Lyme, Oswestry

Liverpool, Birkenhead, Wallasey, Bootle, Crosby, Bebington, Ellesmere Port, Mold, Wrexham, Llangollen, Corwen, Denbigh, St. Asaph, Colwyn Bay, Rhyl, Llandudno, Conwy, Bangor, Caernarfon, Blaenau Ffestiniog, Pwllheli, Llanrwst, Holyhead, Amlwch, Anglesey

Isle of Man, Douglas, Peel, Ramsey, Calf of Man, Point of Ayre

Belfast, Bangor, Larne, Newtownards, Dundrum, Newcastle, Downpatrick, Strangford Lough, Belfast Lough

Cromer, Wells, King's Lynn, Skegness, Louth

Rivers: Tweed, Till, N. Tyne, S. Tyne, Wear, Tees, Swale, Ure, Nidd, Wharfe, Ouse, Derwent, Don, Trent, Witham, Eden, Lune, Ribble, Dee, Severn, Dove, Doon, Nith, Annan, Esk, Ettrick Water

Kielder Res., Windermere, L. Lomond, L. Ryan, Loch Lomond

I. of Walney, Barrow-in-Furness, Fleetwood, Blackpool, Lytham, Southport, Formby, Preston, Chorley, Ormskirk, Lancaster, Morecambe, Workington, Whitehaven, St Bees Hd.

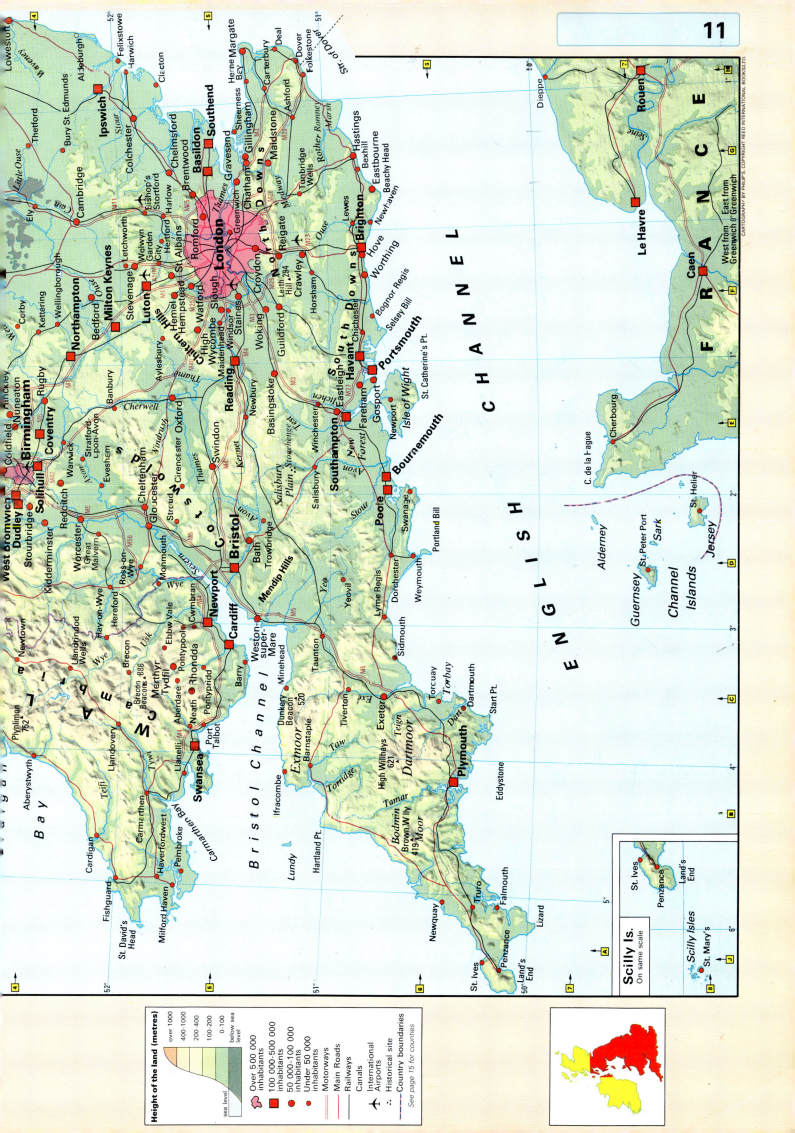

Lowestoft
Lake Denes
Beccles
Thetford
Bury St. Edmunds
Ipswich
Cambridge
Ely
Little Ouse
Witham
Colchester
Chelmsford
Brentwood
Basildon
Southend
Romford
LONDON
Gravesend
Chatham
Gillingham
Maidstone
Margate
Herne Bay
Canterbury
Deal
Dover
Folkestone
Ashford
Romney Marsh
Hastings
Bexhill
Eastbourne
Beachy Head
Herne
Greenwich
North Downs
Reigate
Crawley
Tunbridge Wells
Rother
Medway
Lewes
Ouse
Brighton
Hove
Worthing
Newhaven
Harwich
Clacton
Felixstowe
Aldeburgh
Stour

Milton Keynes
Luton
Stevenage
Welwyn Garden City
Hertford
St. Albans
Hemel Hempstead
Watford
Slough
Windsor
Staines
Woking
Guildford
Leith Hill 294
Dorking
Horsham
Chichester
Havant
Portsmouth
Gosport
Fareham
Bognor Regis
Selsey Bill
Isle of Wight
St. Catherine's Pt.
South Downs
Chiltern Hills

Northampton
Bedford
Wellingborough
Kettering
Corby
Aylesbury
High Wycombe
Maidenhead
Reading
Newbury
Basingstoke
Winchester
Eastleigh
Southampton
New Forest
Newport
Bournemouth
Poole
Swanage

Rugby
Coventry
Birmingham
Solihull
West Bromwich
Dudley
Stourbridge
Kidderminster
Redditch
Warwick
Banbury
Stratford-upon-Avon
Evesham
Worcester
Great Malvern
Cheltenham
Stroud
Gloucester
Oxford
Cirencester
Swindon
Bath
Trowbridge
Bristol
Newport
Cardiff
Weston-super-Mare
Bridgwater
Taunton
Minehead
Exmoor
Ilfracombe
Barnstaple
Dunkery Beacon 520
Tiverton
Exeter
Dartmoor
High Willhays 621
Brown Willy 419
Bodmin Moor
Plymouth
Torquay
Torbay
Dartmouth
Start Pt.
Eddystone
Newquay
Truro
Falmouth
Lizard
Land's End
St. Ives
Penzance

Cherwell
Avon
Severn
Wye
Usk
Monmouth
Ross-on-Wye
Hereford
Hay-on-Wye
Brecon
Brecon Beacons 886
Merthyr Tydfil
Aberdare
Rhondda
Pontypridd
Pontypool
Ebbw Vale
Cwmbran
Neath
Llanelli
Swansea
Port Talbot
Barry
Carmarthen
Haverfordwest
Milford Haven
Pembroke
Fishguard
St. David's Head
Aberystwyth
Newtown
Llandrindod Wells
Plynlimon 752
Llandovery
Teifi
Tywi
Towy
Cardigan
Cardigan Bay
WALES
Newport

Salisbury
Salisbury Plain
Stonehenge
Mendip Hills
Yeo
Stour
Avon
Dorchester
Weymouth
Portland Bill
Lyme Regis
Sidmouth
Yeovil
Taw
Torridge
Tamar
Teign
Exe

ENGLISH CHANNEL
Bristol Channel
Lundy
Hartland Pt.

FRANCE
Dieppe
Rouen
Le Havre
Caen
Cherbourg
C. de la Hague
Seine

CHANNEL
Alderney
Guernsey
St. Peter Port
Sark
St. Helier
Jersey
Channel Islands

West from Greenwich 0° East from Greenwich
CARTOGRAPHY BY PHILIP'S. COPYRIGHT REED INTERNATIONAL BOOKS LTD.

52
5
5
51
50

G
F
E
D
C
B
A
J
7
6
5
4

Height of the land (metres)
over 1000
400-1000
200-400
100-200
0-100
below sea level
sea level

Over 500 000 inhabitants
100 000-500 000 inhabitants
50 000-100 000 inhabitants
Under 50 000 inhabitants
Motorways
Main Roads
Railways
Canals
International Airports
Historical site
Country boundaries
See page 15 for counties

Orkney Is.
On same scale

Shetland Is.
On same scale

Scale 1:2 000 000
1 cm on the map = 20 km on the ground

0   50km   100km   150km   200km

CARTOGRAPHY BY PHILIP'S. COPYRIGHT REED INTERNATIONAL BOOKS LTD.

Scale 1:4 600 000   1 cm on the map = 46 km on the ground

HIGHEST MOUNTAINS, LARGEST LAKES & LONGEST RIVERS		
England		
Scafell Pike		978m
Windermere		14.8km²
Thames		346km
Severn		354km
Wales		
Snowdon		1085m
Trawsfynydd L.		4.9km²
Tywi		109km
Severn		354km
Scotland		
Ben Nevis		1347m
Loch Lomond		69.9km²
Tay		188km
Northern Ireland		
Slieve Donard		852m
Lough Neagh		396.0km²
Bann		128.7km
Ireland		
Carrauntoohil		1042m
Lough Corrib		176.0km²
Shannon		354km

Shetland Is.

Fair I.

Orkney Is.

C. Wrath   Pentland Firth   Duncansby Hd.

Lewis

St. Kilda   Harris

Outer Hebrides

North Uist

South Uist   Skye   1182   Moray Firth   Kinnairds Head

Rhum   Spey   Cairn Gorm 1245

Coll   Ben Nevis   1347   Dee

Inner Hebrides   Tiree   Mull   1724   1214

North West Highlands

Grampian Mts.

Jura   L. Lomond   Tay

Islay   Firth of Forth

ATLANTIC   Arran   Clyde

OCEAN   Firth of Clyde   Southern Uplands   Tweed   830   The Cheviot 816

North Channel   843   The Cheviot

Malin Hd.   554   Solway Firth   Tyne

752   683   Mull of Galloway   Scafell Pike 978   893   Tees   454

Ireland   Bann   Lake District   Pennines   Flamborough Hd.

Donegal Bay   L. Erne   Neagh   Isle of Man   Windermere

644   Mourne Mts.   IRISH SEA   The Peak 636   Aire   Humber

Achill I.   Slieve Donard 852   Liverpool Bay   Mersey

819   L. Ree   Boyne   Anglesey   Dee   Trent   The Wash

L. Corrib   Liffey   Snowdon 1085   NORTH SEA

Galway Bay   Wicklow Mts. 926   Trawsfynydd L.   The Fens

Aran Is.   L. Derg   Cambrian Mts.   315

Shannon   Barrow   Suir   Cardigan Bay   Severn   Avon

953   920   Blackwater   Wye   330   Cotswolds   Chiltern Hills

Dingle Bay   Carrauntoohil 1041   Tywi   Brecon Beacons 886   297   Thames   North Foreland

Bantry Bay   St. George's Channel   St. David's Hd.   Salisbury Plain   North Downs

C. Clear   Bristol Channel   South Downs   Beachy Hd.   Strait of Dover

CELTIC   Exmoor   618 Dartmoor   Lyme Bay   Isle of Wight

SEA   Land's End   Portland Bill   ENGLISH CHANNEL

Scilly Is.   Lizard   France

Channel Is.   Seine

Guernsey   Somme

Jersey   West from Greenwich 0° East from Greenwich

Great Britain

ATLANTIC OCEAN

North Channel

COPYRIGHT, GEORGE PHILIP 5?

CARTOGRAPHY BY PHILIP'S COPYRIGHT REED INTERNATIONAL BOOKS LTD

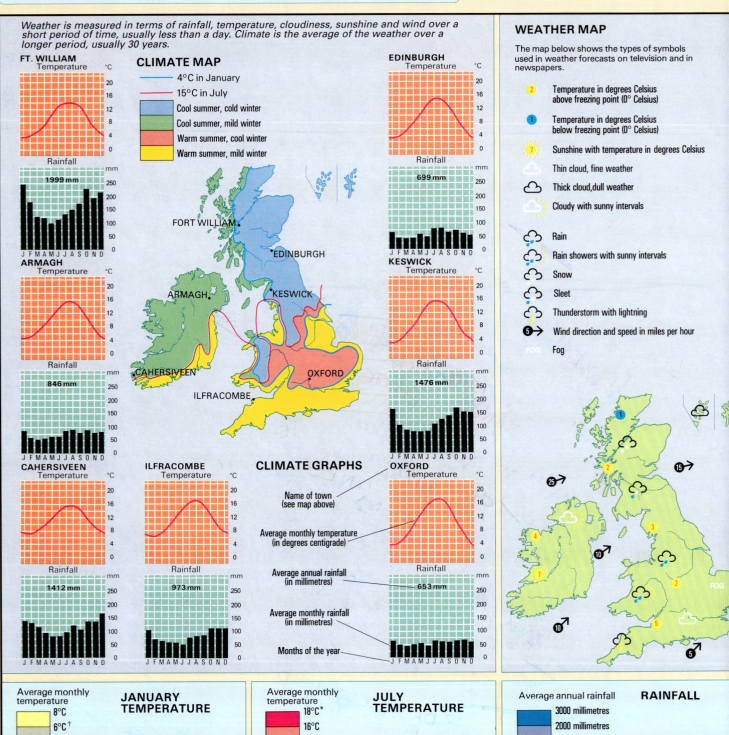

Weather is measured in terms of rainfall, temperature, cloudiness, sunshine and wind over a short period of time, usually less than a day. Climate is the average of the weather over a longer period, usually 30 years.

CLIMATE MAP

- 4°C in January
- 15°C in July
- Cool summer, cold winter
- Cool summer, mild winter
- Warm summer, cool winter
- Warm summer, mild winter

FT. WILLIAM
Temperature °C
20 16 12 8 4 0

Rainfall mm
1999 mm
250 200 150 100 50 0
J F M A M J J A S O N D

ARMAGH
Temperature °C
20 16 12 8 4 0

Rainfall mm
846 mm
250 200 150 100 50 0
J F M A M J J A S O N D

CAHERSIVEEN
Temperature °C
20 16 12 8 4 0

Rainfall mm
1412 mm
250 200 150 100 50 0
J F M A M J J A S O N D

ILFRACOMBE
Temperature °C
20 16 12 8 4 0

Rainfall mm
973 mm
250 200 150 100 50 0
J F M A M J J A S O N D

EDINBURGH
Temperature °C
20 16 12 8 4 0

Rainfall mm
699 mm
250 200 150 100 50 0
J F M A M J J A S O N D

KESWICK
Temperature °C
20 16 12 8 4 0

Rainfall mm
1476 mm
250 200 150 100 50 0
J F M A M J J A S O N D

OXFORD
Temperature °C
20 16 12 8 4 0

Rainfall mm
653 mm
250 200 150 100 50 0
J F M A M J J A S O N D

CLIMATE GRAPHS

- Name of town (see map above)
- Average monthly temperature (in degrees centigrade)
- Average annual rainfall (in millimetres)
- Average monthly rainfall (in millimetres)
- Months of the year

Map labels: FORT WILLIAM, EDINBURGH, KESWICK, ARMAGH, CAHERSIVEEN, ILFRACOMBE, OXFORD

WEATHER MAP

The map below shows the types of symbols used in weather forecasts on television and in newspapers.

- 2 Temperature in degrees Celsius above freezing point (0° Celsius)
- 1 Temperature in degrees Celsius below freezing point (0° Celsius)
- 7 Sunshine with temperature in degrees Celsius
- Thin cloud, fine weather
- Thick cloud, dull weather
- Cloudy with sunny intervals
- Rain
- Rain showers with sunny intervals
- Snow
- Sleet
- Thunderstorm with lightning
- 5 Wind direction and speed in miles per hour
- FOG Fog

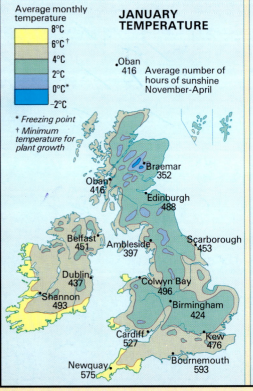

JANUARY TEMPERATURE

Average monthly temperature
- 8°C
- 6°C †
- 4°C
- 2°C
- 0°C *
- -2°C

* Freezing point
† Minimum temperature for plant growth

Oban 416 — Average number of hours of sunshine November-April

Braemar 352
Oban 416
Edinburgh 488
Belfast 451
Ambleside 397
Scarborough 453
Dublin 437
Shannon 493
Colwyn Bay 496
Birmingham 424
Cardiff 527
Kew 476
Newquay 575
Bournemouth 593

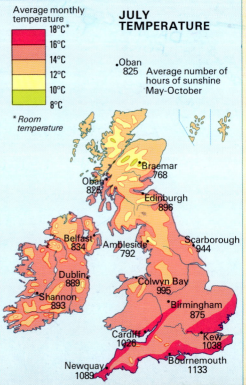

JULY TEMPERATURE

Average monthly temperature
- 18°C *
- 16°C
- 14°C
- 12°C
- 10°C
- 8°C

* Room temperature

Oban 825 — Average number of hours of sunshine May-October

Braemar 768
Oban 825
Edinburgh 896
Belfast 834
Ambleside 792
Scarborough 944
Dublin 889
Shannon 893
Colwyn Bay 995
Birmingham 875
Cardiff 1026
Kew 1038
Newquay 1089
Bournemouth 1133

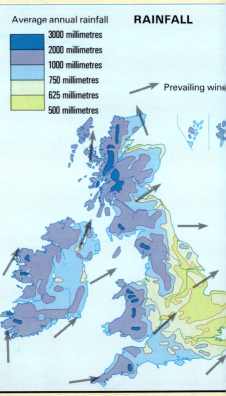

RAINFALL

Average annual rainfall
- 3000 millimetres
- 2000 millimetres
- 1000 millimetres
- 750 millimetres
- 625 millimetres
- 500 millimetres

Prevailing wind

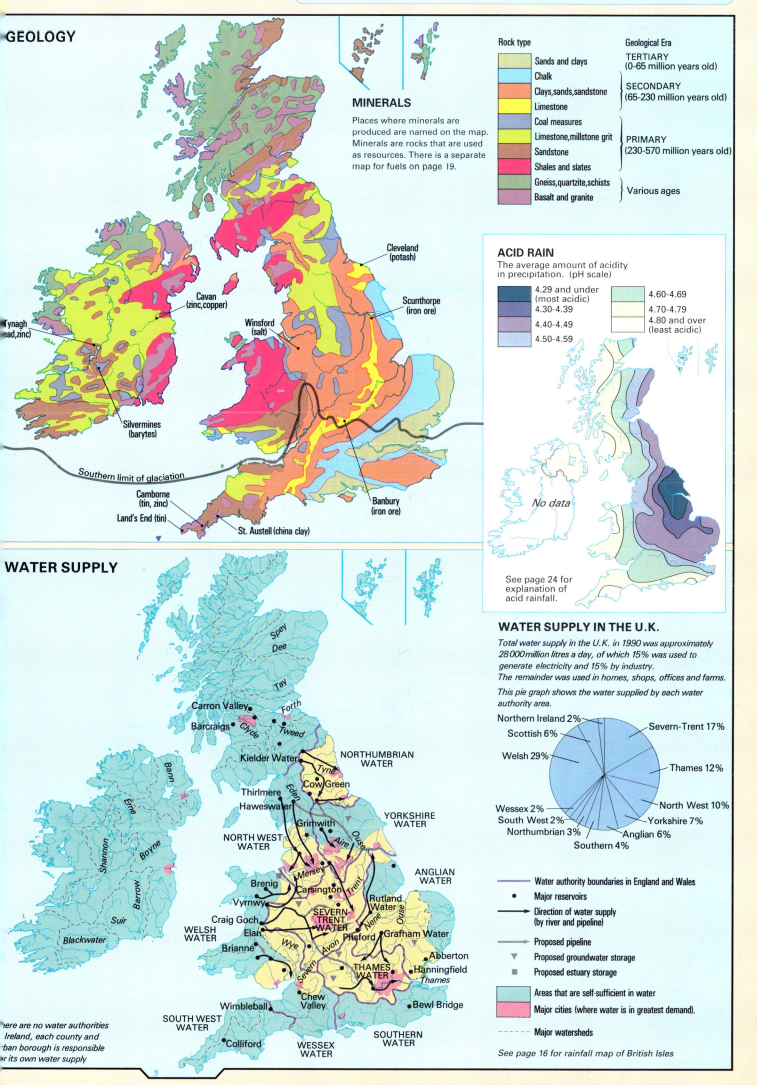

GEOLOGY

MINERALS

Places where minerals are produced are named on the map. Minerals are rocks that are used as resources. There is a separate map for fuels on page 19.

Rock type		Geological Era
	Sands and clays	TERTIARY (0-65 million years old)
	Chalk	
	Clays,sands,sandstone	SECONDARY (65-230 million years old)
	Limestone	
	Coal measures	PRIMARY (230-570 million years old)
	Limestone,millstone grit	
	Sandstone	
	Shales and slates	
	Gneiss,quartzite,schists	Various ages
	Basalt and granite	

Cleveland (potash)

Scunthorpe (iron ore)

Cavan (zinc,copper)

Winsford (salt)

Tynagh (lead,zinc)

Silvermines (barytes)

Camborne (tin, zinc)

Land's End (tin)

St. Austell (china clay)

Banbury (iron ore)

Southern limit of glaciation

ACID RAIN

The average amount of acidity in precipitation. (pH scale)

4.29 and under (most acidic)	4.60-4.69
4.30-4.39	4.70-4.79
4.40-4.49	4.80 and over (least acidic)
4.50-4.59	

No data

See page 24 for explanation of acid rainfall.

WATER SUPPLY

WATER SUPPLY IN THE U.K.

Total water supply in the U.K. in 1990 was approximately 28 000 million litres a day, of which 15% was used to generate electricity and 15% by industry. The remainder was used in homes, shops, offices and farms.

This pie graph shows the water supplied by each water authority area.

Northern Ireland 2%
Scottish 6%
Welsh 29%
Wessex 2%
South West 2%
Northumbrian 3%
Southern 4%
Anglian 6%
Yorkshire 7%
North West 10%
Thames 12%
Severn-Trent 17%

Spey
Dee
Tay
Forth
Tweed
Clyde
Carron Valley
Barcraigs
Kielder Water
NORTHUMBRIAN WATER
Tyne
Cow Green
Thirlmere
Haweswater
Eden
YORKSHIRE WATER
Grimwith
NORTH WEST WATER
Aire
Ouse
Mersey
Trent
ANGLIAN WATER
Brenig
Carsington
Vyrnwy
Rutland Water
Nene
Ouse
SEVERN-TRENT WATER
Craig Goch
Elan
Pitsford
Grafham Water
WELSH WATER
Brianne
Wye
Avon
Severn
THAMES WATER
Abberton
Hanningfield
Thames
Chew Valley
Bewl Bridge
Wimbleball
SOUTH WEST WATER
Colliford
WESSEX WATER
SOUTHERN WATER
Bann
Erne
Shannon
Boyne
Barrow
Suir
Blackwater

	Water authority boundaries in England and Wales
●	Major reservoirs
→	Direction of water supply (by river and pipeline)
	Proposed pipeline
▼	Proposed groundwater storage
■	Proposed estuary storage
	Areas that are self-sufficient in water
	Major cities (where water is in greatest demand).
- - -	Major watersheds

here are no water authorities Ireland, each county and ban borough is responsible r its own water supply

See page 16 for rainfall map of British Isles

18 British Isles : Food

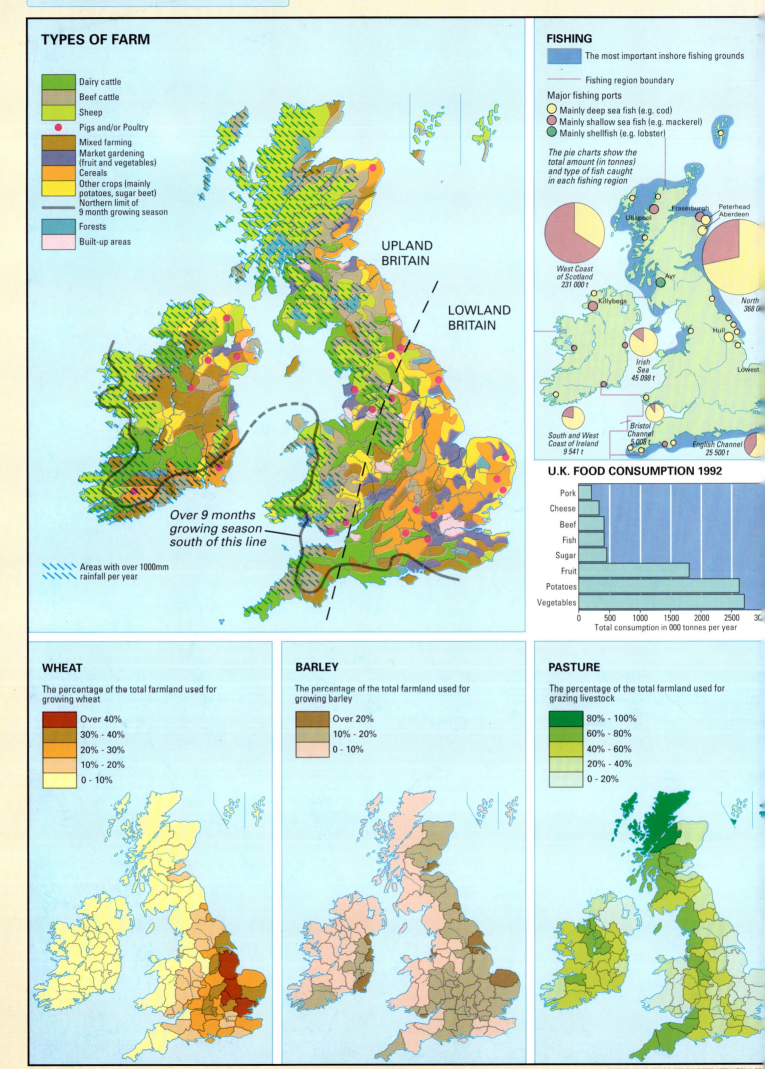

TYPES OF FARM

- Dairy cattle
- Beef cattle
- Sheep
- ● Pigs and/or Poultry
- Mixed farming
- Market gardening (fruit and vegetables)
- Cereals
- Other crops (mainly potatoes, sugar beet)
- Northern limit of 9 month growing season
- Forests
- Built-up areas

UPLAND BRITAIN

LOWLAND BRITAIN

Over 9 months growing season south of this line

Areas with over 1000mm rainfall per year

FISHING

- The most important inshore fishing grounds
- Fishing region boundary

Major fishing ports
- ○ Mainly deep sea fish (e.g. cod)
- ● Mainly shallow sea fish (e.g. mackerel)
- ● Mainly shellfish (e.g. lobster)

The pie charts show the total amount (in tonnes) and type of fish caught in each fishing region

Ullapool
Fraserburgh
Peterhead
Aberdeen
Ayr
Killybegs
Hull

West Coast of Scotland 231 000 t

North 368 0

Irish Sea 45 098 t

Lowest

South and West Coast of Ireland 9 541 t

Bristol Channel 5 008 t

English Channel 25 500 t

U.K. FOOD CONSUMPTION 1992

Pork
Cheese
Beef
Fish
Sugar
Fruit
Potatoes
Vegetables

0   500   1000   1500   2000   2500   30

Total consumption in 000 tonnes per year

WHEAT

The percentage of the total farmland used for growing wheat

- Over 40%
- 30% - 40%
- 20% - 30%
- 10% - 20%
- 0 - 10%

BARLEY

The percentage of the total farmland used for growing barley

- Over 20%
- 10% - 20%
- 0 - 10%

PASTURE

The percentage of the total farmland used for grazing livestock

- 80% - 100%
- 60% - 80%
- 40% - 60%
- 20% - 40%
- 0 - 20%

U.K. ENERGY PRODUCTION

This graph shows the production totals for the four main sources of energy in the U.K. since 1964. All figures are shown as the amount of energy that would have been produced if coal had been burnt. This figure is given in millions of tonnes of coal.

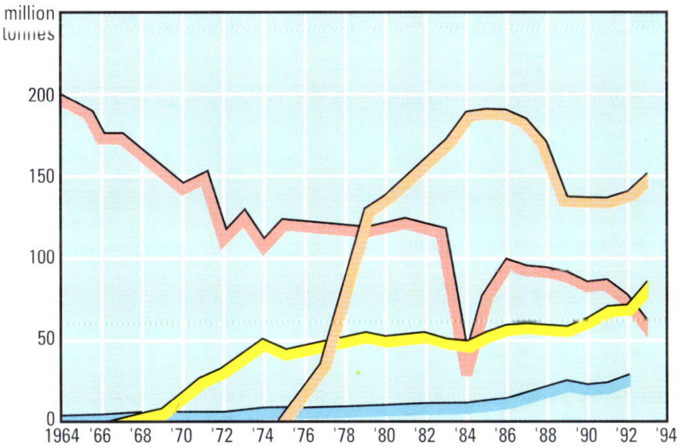

- Coal
- Oil
- Hydro and Nuclear Electricity
- Natural Gas

million tonnes

200
150
100
50
0

1964 '66 '68 '70 '72 '74 '76 '78 '80 '82 '84 '86 '88 '90 '92 '94

ENERGY SOURCES

- Coalfield
- Coal-fired* power station (over 1000MW)
- Peat-cutting area in Ireland
- Oilfield
- Oil pipeline (with terminal)
- Oil-fired* power station (over 1000MW in U.K., over 500MW in Ireland)
- Gasfield
- Gas pipeline (with terminal)
- International dividing line
- Hydro-electric power station (over 40MW)
- Pumped storage scheme
- Nuclear power station (over 1000MW)

* Oil-fired and Coal-fired refers to the fuel that is being burnt to generate the electricity

NORWAY

Statfjord Oilfield
Brent Oilfield
Shetland Is.
Sullom Voe Oil Terminal
Frigg
NORWEGIAN SECTOR
Orkney Is.
Flotta Oil Terminal
Piper Oilfield
NORTH SEA
Beatrice
ATLANTIC OCEAN
Nigg
Fasnakyle
Foyers
St. Fergus
Peterhead
Cruden Bay
Forties Oilfield
U.K. SECTOR
Ekofisk Oilfield
U.K. SECTOR
Frrochty
Clunie
Rannoch
Lochay
Cruachan
Sloy
Longannet
Inverkip
Cockenzie
Torness
Hunterston
Blyth
IRISH SECTOR
Ballylumford
Maleen's Hall
Sellafield
Teesside
Heysham
DUTCH SECTOR
Morecambe Gasfield
Esmond
Ferrybridge
Drax
Poolbeg
Wylfa
Eggborough
Turlough Hill
Fiddler's Ferry
West Burton
Ardnacrusha
Dinorwic
Ince
Cottam
Ffestiniog
Ratcliffe-on-Soar
Bacton
Leman Bank Gasfield
Aghada
Rugeley
Drakelow
Inniscarra
Rheidol
Kinsale Head Gasfield
Pembroke
Didcot
Tilbury
Celtic Sea
Aberthaw
West Thurrock
Grain
Kingsnorth
Hinkley Point
Wytch Farm Oilfield
Fawley
Dungeness
Sizewell
English Channel
BELGIUM
FRANCE
Irish Sea

COALMINING 1966 – 1994

	1966	1993
Production (million tonnes)	188	68
Coalminers (thousands)	520	20
Number of deep mines	483	31

In December 1994, after 48 years of State ownership, Britain's deep mines and opencast sites returned to the private sector. The five regional mining companies and their acquisitions are shown below.

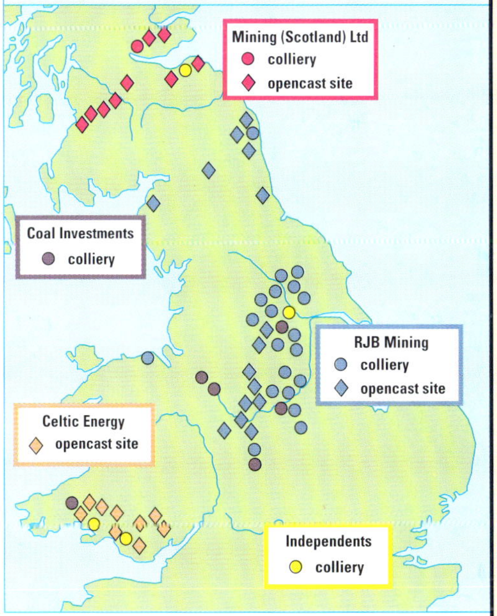

Mining (Scotland) Ltd
- colliery
- opencast site

Coal Investments
- colliery

RJB Mining
- colliery
- opencast site

Celtic Energy
- opencast site

Independents
- colliery

SOURCES OF ENERGY USED IN THE U.K.

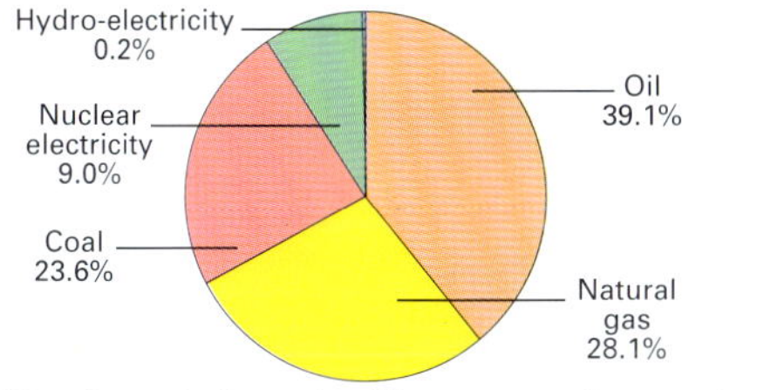

- Hydro-electricity 0.2%
- Nuclear electricity 9.0%
- Coal 23.6%
- Oil 39.1%
- Natural gas 28.1%

The pie graph shows the different types of energy that were used in 1993. The U.K. used 84% of the oil it produced from the North Sea and other U.K. Oilfields. The rest of the oil was exported.

ELECTRICITY 1981 - 1992

Fuel used in the generation of electricity, 1981 and 1992

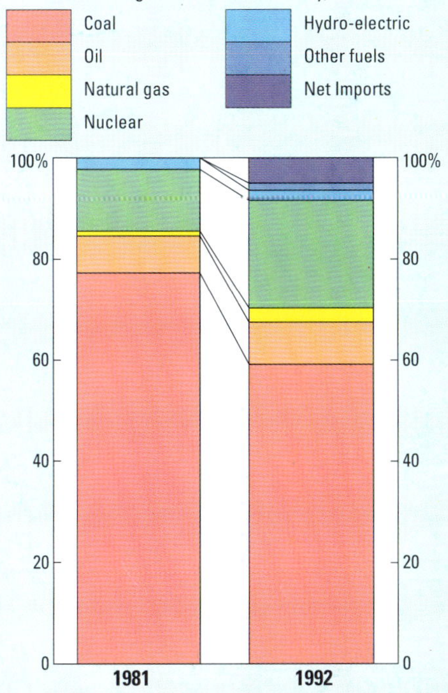

- Coal
- Oil
- Natural gas
- Nuclear
- Hydro-electric
- Other fuels
- Net Imports

100%
80
60
40
20
0

1981 **1992**

The use of coal in the generation of electricity has dropped over the 11 year period, while the use of nuclear power has increased by 76%.

20 British Isles : Trade and Industry

PORTS

The weight of goods handled in millions of tonnes, 1991

5 10 20   50 millions of tonnes

● Mainly fuel oils   ● Mainly general cargo

*The main container ports

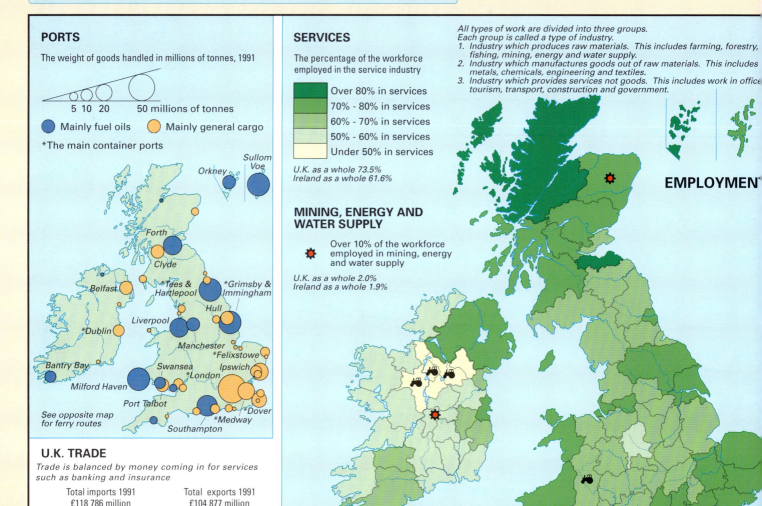

Orkney
Sullom Voe
Forth
Clyde
Belfast
*Tees & Hartlepool
*Grimsby & Immingham
Hull
*Dublin
Liverpool
Manchester
*Felixstowe
Bantry Bay
Swansea
Ipswich
Milford Haven
*London
Port Talbot
*Dover
*Medway
Southampton

See opposite map for ferry routes

U.K. TRADE

Trade is balanced by money coming in for services such as banking and insurance

Total imports 1991
£118 786 million

- Other Goods 5.7%
- Food and Drink 10.4%
- Fuel and Chemicals 15.6%
- Manufactured Goods 32.0%
- Machinery and Transport Equipment 36.3%

Total exports 1991
£104 877 million

- Other Goods 3.6%
- Food and Drink 7.4%
- Fuel and Chemicals 20.0%
- Manufactured Goods 27.4%
- Machinery and Transport Equipment 41.6%

SERVICES

The percentage of the workforce employed in the service industry

- Over 80% in services
- 70% - 80% in services
- 60% - 70% in services
- 50% - 60% in services
- Under 50% in services

U.K. as a whole 73.5%
Ireland as a whole 61.6%

MINING, ENERGY AND WATER SUPPLY

✳ Over 10% of the workforce employed in mining, energy and water supply

U.K. as a whole 2.0%
Ireland as a whole 1.9%

FARMING, FORESTRY AND FISHING

🚜 Over 10% of the workforce employed in farming, forestry and fishing

U.K. as a whole 1.4%
Ireland as a whole 15.0%

All types of work are divided into three groups. Each group is called a type of industry.
1. Industry which produces raw materials. This includes farming, forestry, fishing, mining, energy and water supply.
2. Industry which manufactures goods out of raw materials. This includes metals, chemicals, engineering and textiles.
3. Industry which provides services not goods. This includes work in offices, tourism, transport, construction and government.

EMPLOYMENT

EMPLOYMENT IN MANUFACTURING INDUSTRY

The percentage of the workforce employed in manufacturing in 1991. (Ireland 1989)

- Over 30%
- 25% - 30%
- 20% - 25%
- 15% - 20%
- 12.5% - 15%
- Under 12.5%

LOCATION OF MANUFACTURING INDUSTRY

Heavy Industry
- ▲ Chemicals
- ■ Iron and Steel
- ● Motor vehicles

Light Industry
- ◆ Electrical Engineering

40% of employment in electrical engineering in the U.K. is in the South East

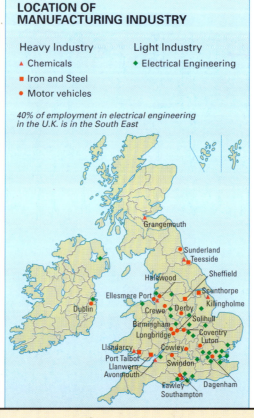

Grangemouth
Sunderland
Teesside
Halewood
Sheffield
Ellesmere Port
Scunthorpe
Killingholme
Dublin
Crewe
Derby
Solihull
Birmingham
Coventry
Longbridge
Luton
Llandarcy
Cowley
Port Talbot
Swindon
Llanwern
Avonmouth
Dagenham
Fawley
Southampton

UNEMPLOYMENT

The percentage of the workforce unemployed in 1994. (Ireland 1986)

- Over 17.5%
- 15% - 17.5%
- 12.5% - 15%
- 10% - 12.5%
- 7.5% - 10%
- Under 7.5%

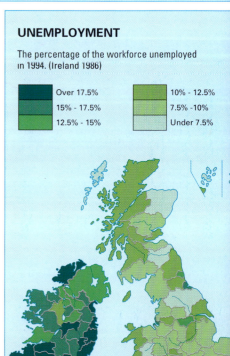

LEISURE

- National Parks
- Areas of Outstanding Natural Beauty
- National Scenic Areas in Scotland
- Forest Parks and Special Protected Areas
- Long Distance Footpaths
- ● Main tourist resorts
- ◆ Major tourist attractions
- Built-up areas

TRAVEL

- Motorways
- Motorways being built
- Other important roads
- Main Intercity railways
- Main ferry routes
- Channel Tunnel
- ● International airports

HOLIDAYS ABROAD

Thousands of U.K. visitors in 1992 to -

France	7 875
Spain	5 665
U.S.A.	2 414
Irish Rep.	2 065
Greece	1 906
Germany	1 766
Netherlands	1 362
Portugal	1 229
Italy	1 215
Cyprus	932
Belgium	924
Austria	637
Switzerland	624

VISITORS FROM ABROAD

Thousands of visitors to the U.K. in 1992 from -

U.S.A.	2 690
France	2 477
Germany	2 257
Irish Rep.	1 299
Netherlands	994
Italy	777
Belgium	768
Spain	678
Canada	613
Japan	534

INCOME FROM TOURISM

Total income from tourism 1992
U.K. £18.1 billion
Ireland £12.2 billion

The percentage of total U.K. income from tourism by region in 1992

- Over 25%
- 10% - 25%
- 5% - 10%
- 2.5% - 5%
- 0 - 2.5%

COPYRIGHT GEORGE PHILIP LTD.

POPULATION FACTS

U.K. Population 1993	58 191 000
of which England	48 533 000
Scotland	5 120 200
Wales	2 906 000
N. Ireland	1 632 000
Ireland Population 1994	3 570 700

AGE STRUCTURE OF THE U.K. IN 1901 AND 1991

The age structure shows how old people are and the percentage in each age group that is male and female. The diagram is called a population pyramid. For example, in 1901, 20% of the female population was aged between 10-19. In 1991, about 12% were in this group.

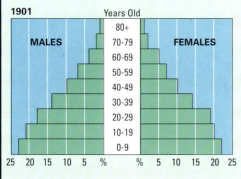

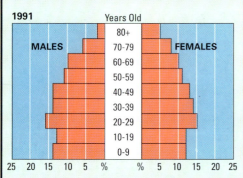

POPULATION DENSITY

Number of people per square kilometre in 1992 (Ireland 1991)

- Over 1000
- 500 - 1000
- 200 - 500
- 100 - 200
- 50 - 100
- 25 - 50
- Under 25

The average density for the U.K. is 223 people per km². The average density for the Republic of Ireland is 51 people per km².

MAJOR CITIES

Population of major cities

- ● Over 1 000 000
- ■ 400 000 – 1 000 000
- ● 200 000 – 400 000
- • 100 000 – 200 000

YOUNG PEOPLE

The percentage of the population under 15 years old in 1992 (Ireland 1991)

- Over 30%
- 25% - 30%
- 20% - 25%
- 19% - 20%
- 18% - 19%
- Under 18%

% young by country U.K. 20.4% Ireland 31%

OLD PEOPLE

The percentage of the population over pensionable age* in 1992 (Ireland 1991)

- Over 20%
- 17.5% - 20%
- 15% - 17.5%
- 12.5% - 15%
- 10% - 12.5%
- Under 10%

% old by country U.K. 18.3% Ireland 14%

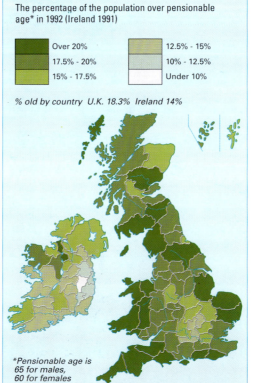

*Pensionable age is 65 for males, 60 for females

POPULATION CHANGE

The percentage change in the number of people betwe 1981 and 1992 (Ireland between 1986 and 1991)

Gain	Loss
Over 15%	0% - 5%
10% - 15%	5% - 10%
5% - 10%	10 - 15%
0% - 5%	

% change by country
U.K. 2.9% gain
Ireland 0.4% loss

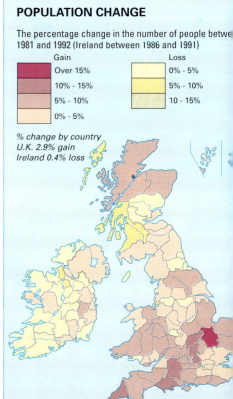

POPULATION

Population density per square kilometre 1993

- Over 300 people per square kilometre
- 200 - 300 people per square kilometre
- 100 - 200 people per square kilometre
- 50 - 100 people per square kilometre
- 10 - 50 people per square kilometre
- Under 10 people per square kilometre

Population increase, 1980 - 1993
The countries which have had the greatest increase in population are:

Albania 27% increase
Iceland 18% increase
Lithuania 11% increase

- ■ Towns with over 5 000 000 inhabitants
- ● Towns with 1 000 000 - 5 000 000 inhabitants

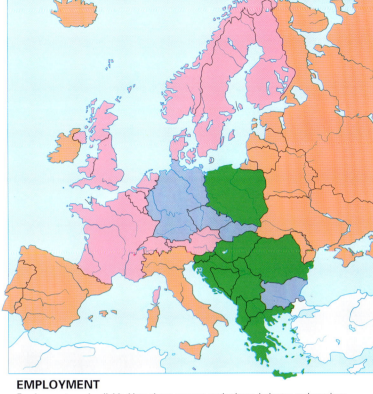

EMPLOYMENT

Employment can be divided into three groups: agriculture, industry and services. This map shows the countries with the highest percentage of people in each group

- Over 20% in agriculture (farming, forestry and fishing)
- Over 40% in industry (includes mining and manufacturing)
- Over 60% in services (includes gas, electricity and water supplies, tourism, banking, education)
- Employment is balanced between the groups (under 20% in agriculture, under 40% in industry, under 60% in services)

TRADE PARTNERS

- E U (European Union)

HQ Brussels

Founder members in 1957:
Belgium, France, Luxembourg, W. Germany, Italy, Netherlands.
UK, Ireland and Denmark joined in 1973, Greece in 1981, Spain and Portugal in 1986, Austria, Finland and Sweden joined in January 1995.

- E F T A (European Free Trade Association)

HQ Geneva. Founded in 1959.
Members in 1995:
Iceland, Liechtenstein, Norway and Switzerland.

- Not a member of any trade organisation

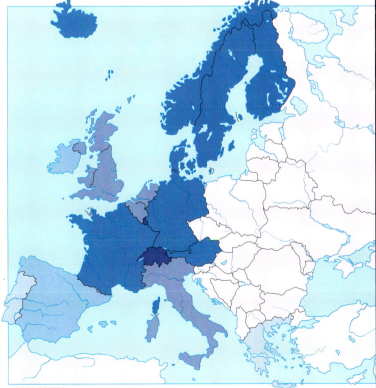

WEALTH

The value of total production divided by population 1991 (US$ per person)

- Over $25 000 per person
- $20 - 25 000 per person
- $15 - 20 000 per person
- $10 - 15 000 per person
- $5 - 10 000 per person
- Under $5 000 per person

Wealthiest countries

Switzerland $33 510 per person
Liechtenstein $33 000 per person
Luxembourg $31 080 per person

Poorest countries

Albania $1 000 per person
Romania $1 340 per person
Poland $1 830 per person

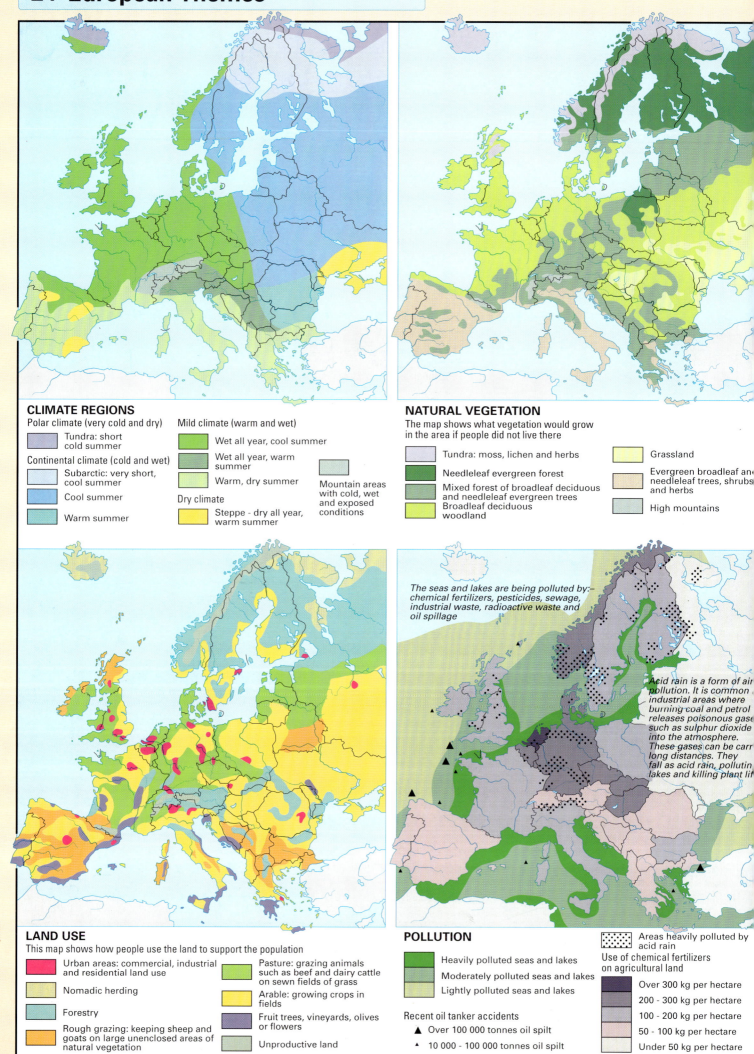

CLIMATE REGIONS

Polar climate (very cold and dry)

- Tundra: short cold summer

Continental climate (cold and wet)

- Subarctic: very short, cool summer
- Cool summer
- Warm summer

Mild climate (warm and wet)

- Wet all year, cool summer
- Wet all year, warm summer
- Warm, dry summer

Dry climate

- Steppe - dry all year, warm summer

- Mountain areas with cold, wet and exposed conditions

NATURAL VEGETATION

The map shows what vegetation would grow in the area if people did not live there

- Tundra: moss, lichen and herbs
- Needleleaf evergreen forest
- Mixed forest of broadleaf deciduous and needleleaf evergreen trees
- Broadleaf deciduous woodland
- Grassland
- Evergreen broadleaf and needleleaf trees, shrubs and herbs
- High mountains

LAND USE

This map shows how people use the land to support the population

- Urban areas: commercial, industrial and residential land use
- Nomadic herding
- Forestry
- Rough grazing: keeping sheep and goats on large unenclosed areas of natural vegetation
- Pasture: grazing animals such as beef and dairy cattle on sewn fields of grass
- Arable: growing crops in fields
- Fruit trees, vineyards, olives or flowers
- Unproductive land

POLLUTION

The seas and lakes are being polluted by:- chemical fertilizers, pesticides, sewage, industrial waste, radioactive waste and oil spillage

Acid rain is a form of air pollution. It is common in industrial areas where burning coal and petrol releases poisonous gases such as sulphur dioxide into the atmosphere. These gases can be carried long distances. They fall as acid rain, polluting lakes and killing plant life.

- Heavily polluted seas and lakes
- Moderately polluted seas and lakes
- Lightly polluted seas and lakes

Recent oil tanker accidents

- ▲ Over 100 000 tonnes oil spilt
- ▴ 10 000 - 100 000 tonnes oil spilt

- Areas heavily polluted by acid rain

Use of chemical fertilizers on agricultural land

- Over 300 kg per hectare
- 200 - 300 kg per hectare
- 100 - 200 kg per hectare
- 50 - 100 kg per hectare
- Under 50 kg per hectare

WORLD MAP SECTION

Below is a slice through the map of Southern Europe on page 10 and 11. It is used here to explain the meaning of the lines, colours and symbols.

Figure/letter reference

Country name

Capital city underlined

Straits and bay names

Town stamp symbol - over 5 000 000 inhabitants

River name

Coastline

Line of longitude

Mountain range

Town stamp symbol - under 1 000 000 inhabitants

Spot height

International boundary

Physical region name

Line of latitude

Island name

Sea

Sea name

Town stamp symbol - 1 000 000 – 5 000 000 inhabitants

HEIGHT OF THE LAND & KEY

These explanation boxes appear on each map to show the height of the land above sea level and to explain some of the features on the map.

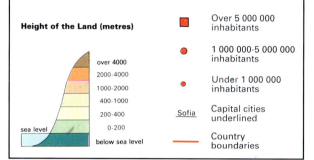

Height of the Land (metres)

over 4000
2000-4000
1000-2000
400-1000
200-400
0-200

sea level

below sea level

☐ Over 5 000 000 inhabitants

● 1 000 000-5 000 000 inhabitants

• Under 1 000 000 inhabitants

Sofia Capital cities underlined

—— Country boundaries

LOCATOR MAP

One of the two styles of map below will appear on each map page. The red area shows how the main map fits into the region around it.

SCALE COMPARISON MAP

Where the map scale allows it, this map appears on map pages at the same scale as the main map, to give an idea of size.

BRITISH ISLES
On same scale

SCALE BAR

Scale 1:50 000 000   1cm on the map = 500km on the ground

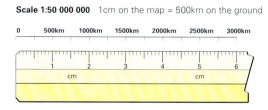

CROSS SECTION

There is a cross section similar to the one below for each continent. These can be found on the relevant map pages.

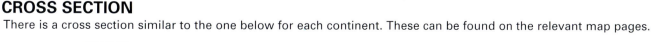
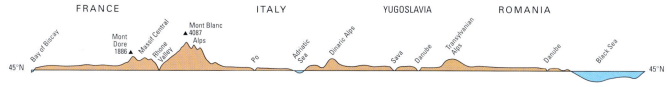

FRANCE   ITALY   YUGOSLAVIA   ROMANIA

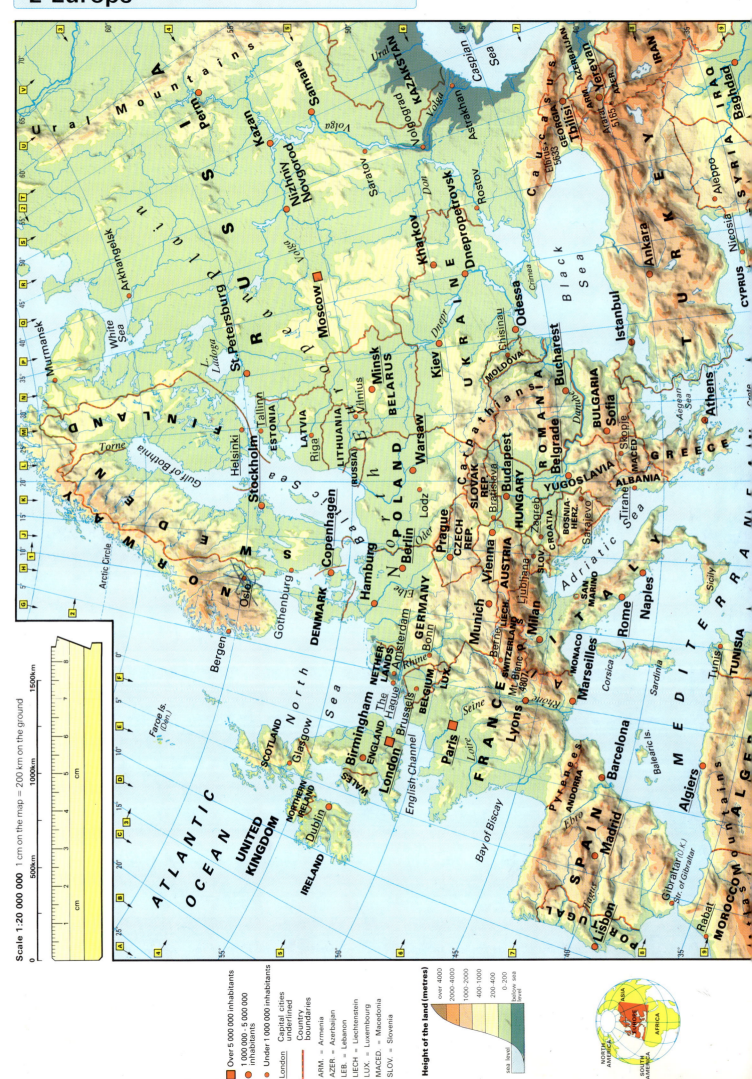

Scandinavia 3

ARCTIC OCEAN

North Cape
Hammerfest
Vardø
Tromsø
Kirkenes
Murmansk
L. Inari
Kola Peninsula
Vesterålen
Lofoten Islands
Narvik
Kebnekaise 2123
Imandra L.
Kandalaksha
Bodø
Kiruna
Torne
Arctic Circle
Rovaniemi
Kemijärvi
White Sea
ATLANTIC OCEAN
Kemi
Arkhangelsk
Luleå
Luleå
Oulu
Kristiansund
Skellefteå
L. Oulu
Kajaani
Karelia
Onega
Ålesund
Trondheim
Östersund
Umeå
Vaasa
Kuopio
Joensuu
L. Onega
Storsjön
Ume
FINLAND
Petrozavodsk
Galdhøpiggen 2469
Jotunhelmen
Sundsvall
Jyväskylä
Bergen
Glåma
Lillehammer
Tampere
L. Saimaa
L. Ladoga
Hardanger Fjord
Mjøsa L.
Gävle
Pori
Lahti
Vyborg
Haugesund
Drammen
Oslo
Åland Is.
Turku
Helsinki
Kotka
St.Petersburg (Leningrad)
Cherepovets
Stavanger
Fredrikstad
Västerås
Uppsala
Gulf of Finland
Kristiansand
Örebro
Stockholm
Tallinn
Novgorod
Rybinsk Res.
Skagerrak
Skagen
Göta Canal
Hiiumaa
ESTONIA
L. Chudskoye
Gothenburg
L. Vänern
Norrköping
Saaremaa
Aalborg
Borås
Linköping
Gulf of Riga
Pskov
RUSSIA
Tver
DENMARK
Jönköping
Gotland
Gotaland
Öland
W. Dvina
Volga
Aarhus
LATVIA
Moscow
Copenhagen
Helsingborg
Riga
Esbjerg
Odense
Malmö
Liepaja
Kaluga
Sjælland
Bornholm
Vitebsk
Smolensk
Kiel Canal
LITHUANIA
Kaunas
Vilnius
Mogilev
Kiel
Rostock
Kaliningrad (RUSSIA)
Minsk
Bryansk
Hamburg
Szczecin
Gdansk
Neman
BELARUS
Bremen
Elbe
Vistula
Bialystok
Gomel
Berlin
Odra
POLAND
Brest
Pripet
Dnepr
Hanover
Poznan
GERMANY
Dortmund
Lodz
Warsaw
Cologne
Leipzig
Dresden
Wroclaw
Lublin
Chernobyl
Rhine
Frankfurt
CZECH REP.
Krakow
Zhitomir
Kiev
Prague
East from Greenwich
UKRAINE

Scale 1:10 000 000   1 cm on the map = 100 km on the ground

0   100km   200km   300km   400km   500km   600km

Height of the land (metres)
over 4000
2000-4000
1000-2000
400-1000
200-400
0-200
sea level
below sea level

Over 5 000 000 inhabitants
1 000 000 - 5 000 000 inhabitants
Under 1 000 000 inhabitants
Helsinki Capital cities underlined
Country boundaries
Ice cap

COPYRIGHT GEORGE PHILIP & SON LTD.

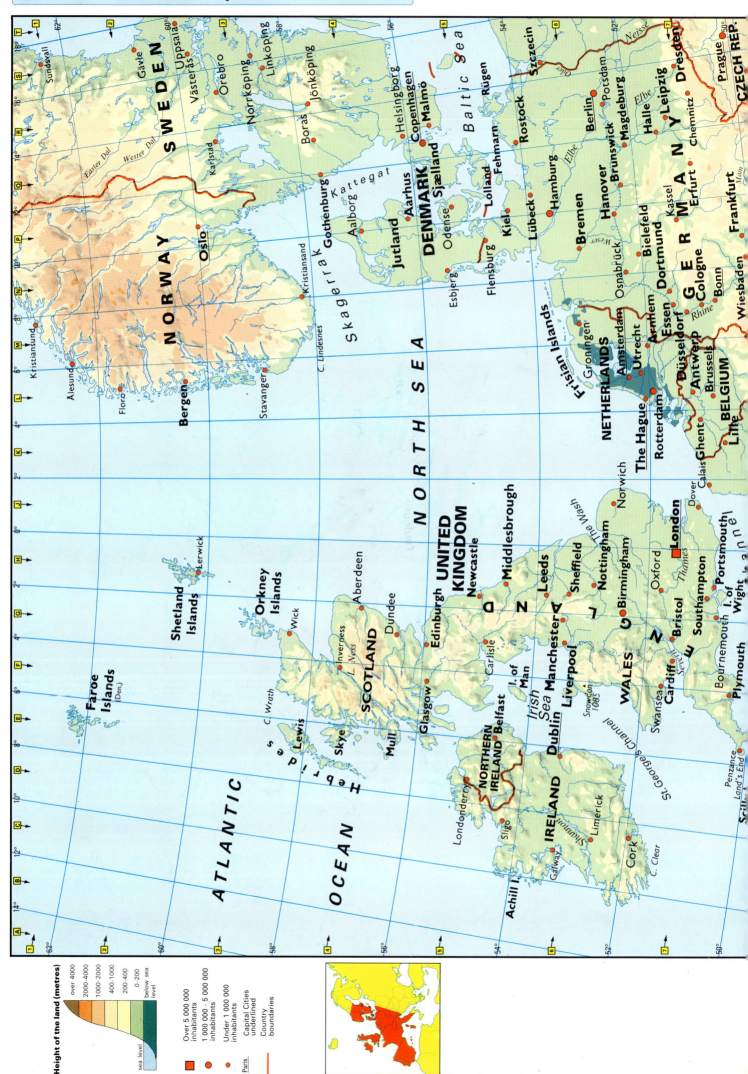

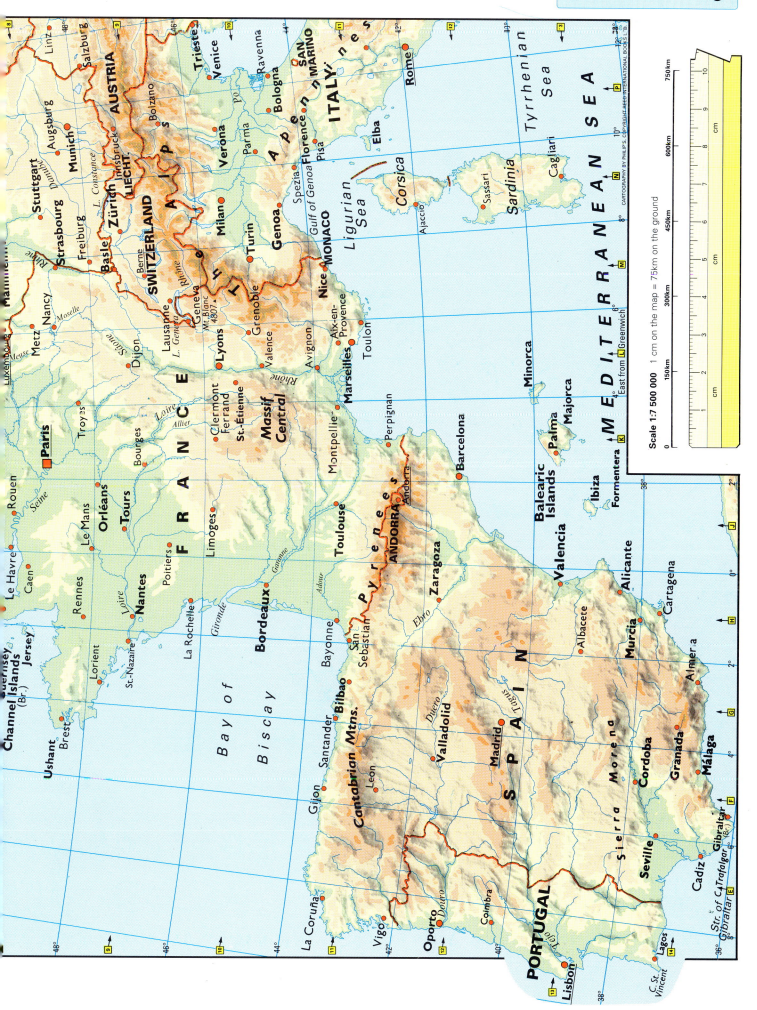

5

Scale 1:7 500 000   1 cm on the map = 75km on the ground

0   150km   300km   450km   600km   750km

CARTOGRAPHY BY PHILIP'S. COPYRIGHT REED INTERNATIONAL BOOKS LTD.

Map labels:

Linz, Salzburg, AUSTRIA, Trieste, Venice, San Marino, Rome, ITALY

Augsburg, Munich, Innsbruck, LIECHT., Bolzano, Verona, Ravenna, Bologna, SAN MARINO

Stuttgart, Strasbourg, Freiburg, Basle, Zürich, SWITZERLAND, ALPS, Milan, Parma, Florence, Pisa, Apennines, Corsica, Tyrrhenian Sea

Mannheim, Rhine, Nancy, Metz, Moselle, Berne, Lausanne, Geneva, L. Geneva, Mt. Blanc 4807, Lyons, Turin, Genoa, Gulf of Genoa, Spezia, Elba, Sassari, Sardinia, Cagliari

Luxembourg, Meuse, Dijon, Saône, Grenoble, Nice, MONACO, Ligurian Sea, Ajaccio

FRANCE, Troyes, Bourges, Allier, Clermont Ferrand, St-Étienne, Valence, Rhône, Avignon, Aix-en-Provence, Marseilles, Toulon

Paris, Loire, Orléans, Tours, Limoges, Massif Central, Montpellier, Perpignan, Minorca, MEDITERRANEAN SEA

Seine, Le Mans, Poitiers, Guéret, Bordeaux, Toulouse, Pyrenees, ANDORRA, Barcelona, Balearic Islands, Palma, Majorca, Ibiza, Formentera

Rouen, Le Havre, Caen, Rennes, Nantes, La Rochelle, Gironde, Adour, Bayonne, San Sebastián, Zaragoza, Ebro, Valencia, Alicante, Cartagena

Channel Islands (Br.), Jersey, Guernsey, Ushant, Brest, Lorient, St-Nazaire, Bay of Biscay, Santander, Bilbao, Cantabrian Mtns., Duero, Valladolid, Madrid, SPAIN, Albacete, Murcia, Almería

La Coruña, Gijón, León, Sierra Morena, Córdoba, Granada, Málaga

Vigo, Oporto, Douro, Coimbra, PORTUGAL, Tagus, Seville, Cádiz, Str. of Gibraltar, Gibraltar (Br.), C. Trafalgar

Lisbon, C. St. Vincent, Lagos

East from Greenwich

ATLANTIC OCEAN

IRELAND

WALES

ENGLAND
Birmingham
Cardiff
Thames
London

English Channel
Channel Is. (U.K.)

Brest

Le Havre

NETHERLANDS
The Hague
Amsterdam
Rotterdam
Dortmund

Bremen
Hamburg
Hanover
Berlin

GERMANY

BELGIUM
Lille
Brussels
Antwerp
Cologne
Bonn

Leipzig
Dresden

LUXEMBOURG
Luxembourg

Frankfurt

Prague
CZEC

Paris
Seine

Strasbourg

Nuremberg
Stuttgart

Linz

Bay of Biscay

Nantes

Loire

FRANCE

Basle
Bern
Zürich

Munich

AUSTR

Bordeaux

Garonne

Lyons

Massif Central

Rhône

Mt. Blanc 4807
L. Geneva
Geneva
SWITZERLAND
Jura

LIECHTENSTEIN

Milan
Turin
L. Garda
Venice
Po

Ljubli
SLOVE
Tries

La Coruña

Cantabrian Mountains

Bilbao
Toulouse

Pyrenees
Pic d'Aneto 3404
ANDORRA

Marseilles

MONACO
Nice

Riviera

Genoa

Bologna
Rimini
SAN MARINO
Florence
Apennines

Oporto
Douro

Valladolid
Duero

Ebro
Zaragoza

Catalonia
Costa Brava

Barcelona

Corsica

Tiber

Gran Sas 2914

PORTUGAL

SPAIN

Madrid
Tajo

Rome
ITALY

Lisbon

Tejo

Valencia

Balearic Is.

Naples
Vesu
Pompei

Sierra Morena

Guadalquivir

Murcia

Palma
Ibiza
Majorca
Minorca

Sardinia

Tyrrhenian Sea

Cagliari

Strombc

Seville

Granada
Malaga
Mulhacén 3478

Costa del Sol

MEDITERRA

Palermo

Sicily
Cata

Tangier
Gibraltar (U.K.)
Strait of Gibraltar

Algiers

Tunis
Carthage

Oran

Valletta
MALTA

Fès

MOROCCO

Atlas Mountains

Constantine

Sfax

A

F

R

ALGERIA

I

C

TUNISIA

A

Tripoli

LIBYA

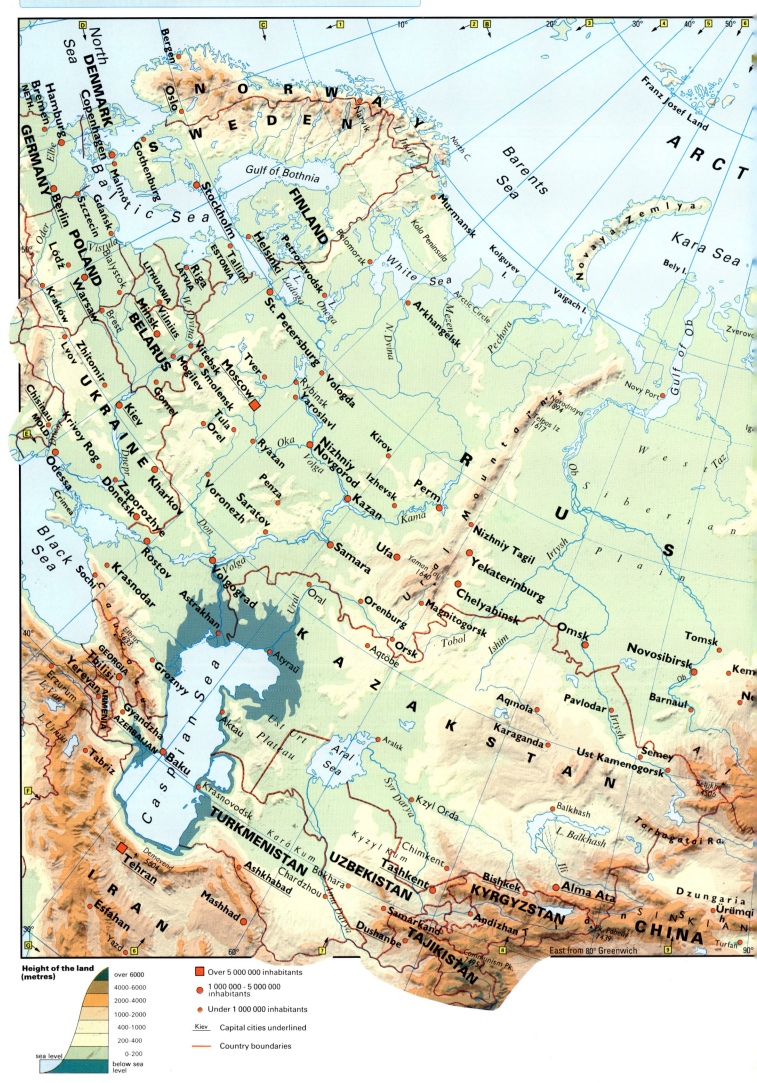

Height of the land (metres)

over 6000	
4000-6000	
2000-4000	
1000-2000	
400-1000	
200-400	
0-200	
below sea level	

sea level

■ Over 5 000 000 inhabitants

● 1 000 000 - 5 000 000 inhabitants

● Under 1 000 000 inhabitants

<u>Kiev</u>   Capital cities underlined

— Country boundaries

9

OCEAN

Komsomolets I.
October Revolution I.
Bolshevik I.
Severnaya
Zemlya
Boris Vilkitski Str.
C. Chelyuskin

East Siberian Sea

Wrangel I.

Anadyr Range

Gulf of Anadyr

Bering Sea

New Siberian Is.

Laptev
Sea

Taimyr
Peninsula

Lyakhov Is.
Dimitri Laptev Str.

Tiksi

Nordvik

Olenek

Khatanga

Kotuy

Norilsk

Yana

Verkhoyansk

Indigirka

Cherskiy Range

Verkhoyansk Range

Kolyma

Nizhne Kolymsk

Kolyma Range

Srednly Khrebet

Anadyr

Anadyr

Gizhiga

Shelekhov
Gulf

Magadan

Okhotsk

Sea of
Okhotsk

Kamchatka
Peninsula

Petropavlovsk-
Kamchatskiy

C e n t r a l
S i b e r i a n
P l a t e a u

Lower Tunguska

Stony Tunguska

Angara

I A

Arctic Circle

Lena

Yakutsk

Olekminsk

Aldan

Aldan

Stanovoy Range

Shantar
Is.

Sakhalin

Aleksandrovsk

Kuril Islands

Yuzhno-Sakhalinsk

Bratsk

Krasnoyarsk

znetsk

Nizhneudinsk

Angara

L. Buikal

Yablonovyy Range

Amur

Komsomolsk

Sikhote Alin

Khabarovsk

Angarsk
Irkutsk

Munku
Sardik
3491

Ulan Ude

Chita

Hailar

Blagoveshchensk

Sungari

Amur

L. Khanka

Hokkaido

Asahikawa

Sapporo

Ubsa
Nur

Khangai
Mts.

Ulan Bator

Qiqihar

Harbin

Vladivostok

Hakodate

MONGOLIA

Gobi

INNER
MONGOLIA

Changchun

Fushun

Shenyang

Anshan

Kirin

Sungari
Res.

Manchuria

NORTH KOREA

Pyongyang

Seoul

SOUTH KOREA

Sea of
Japan

Honshu

Akita

JAPAN

Sendai

Tokyo

Yokohama

Kobe

Osaka

Nagoya

CARTOGRAPHY BY PHILIP'S. COPYRIGHT REED INTERNATIONAL BOOKS LTD.

1:20 000 000   1 cm on the map = 200km on the ground

500km   1000km   1500km   2000km

1   2   3   4   5   6   7   8   9   10
cm   cm   cm

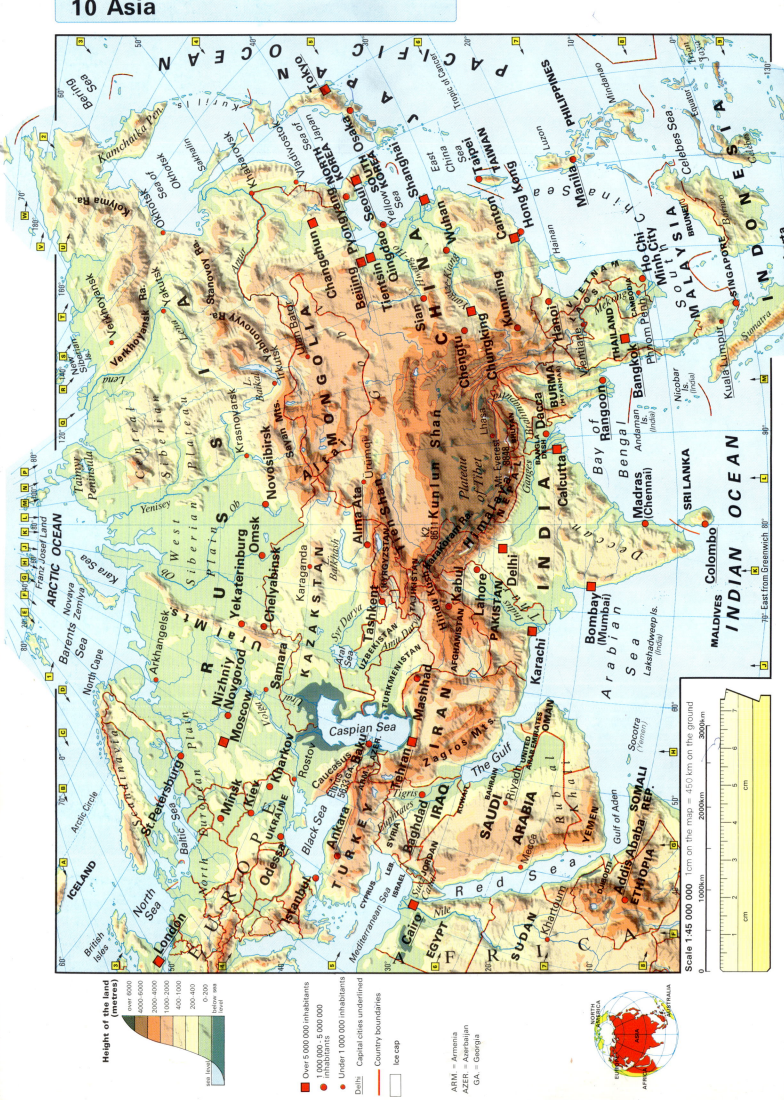

Scale 1:7 500 000   1 cm on the map = 75km on the ground

0   75km   150km   225km   300km   375km   450km

cm   cm

Height of the land (metres)

over 4000
2000-4000
1000-2000
400-1000
200-400
0-200
below sea level
sea level

■ Over 5 000 000 inhabitants
● 1 000 000 - 5 000 000 inhabitants
• Under 1 000 000 inhabitants

Tokyo   Capital cities underlined
──   Country boundaries

CARTOGRAPHY BY PHILIP'S. COPYRIGHT REED INTERNATIONAL BOOKS LTD.

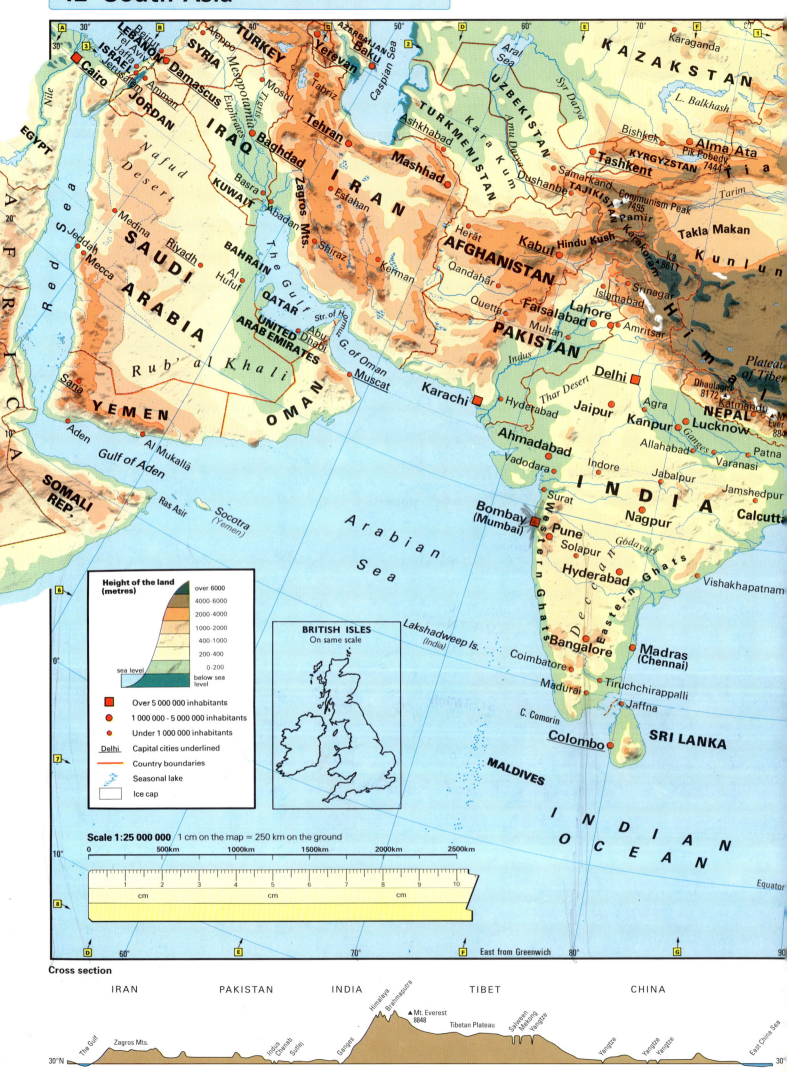

Height of the land (metres)

- over 6000
- 4000-6000
- 2000-4000
- 1000-2000
- 400-1000
- 200-400
- 0-200
- sea level
- below sea level

■ Over 5 000 000 inhabitants
● 1 000 000 - 5 000 000 inhabitants
• Under 1 000 000 inhabitants
<u>Delhi</u> Capital cities underlined
—— Country boundaries
Seasonal lake
Ice cap

BRITISH ISLES
On same scale

Scale 1:25 000 000   1 cm on the map = 250 km on the ground

0   500km   1000km   1500km   2000km   2500km

cm   cm   cm

East from Greenwich

Cross section

IRAN   PAKISTAN   INDIA   TIBET   CHINA

Himalaya
Brahmaputra
▲ Mt. Everest
8848
Tibetan Plateau
Salween Mekong Yangtze

The Gulf   Zagros Mts.   Indus Chenab Sutlej   Ganges   Yangtze Yangtze Yangtze   East China Sea

30°N   30°

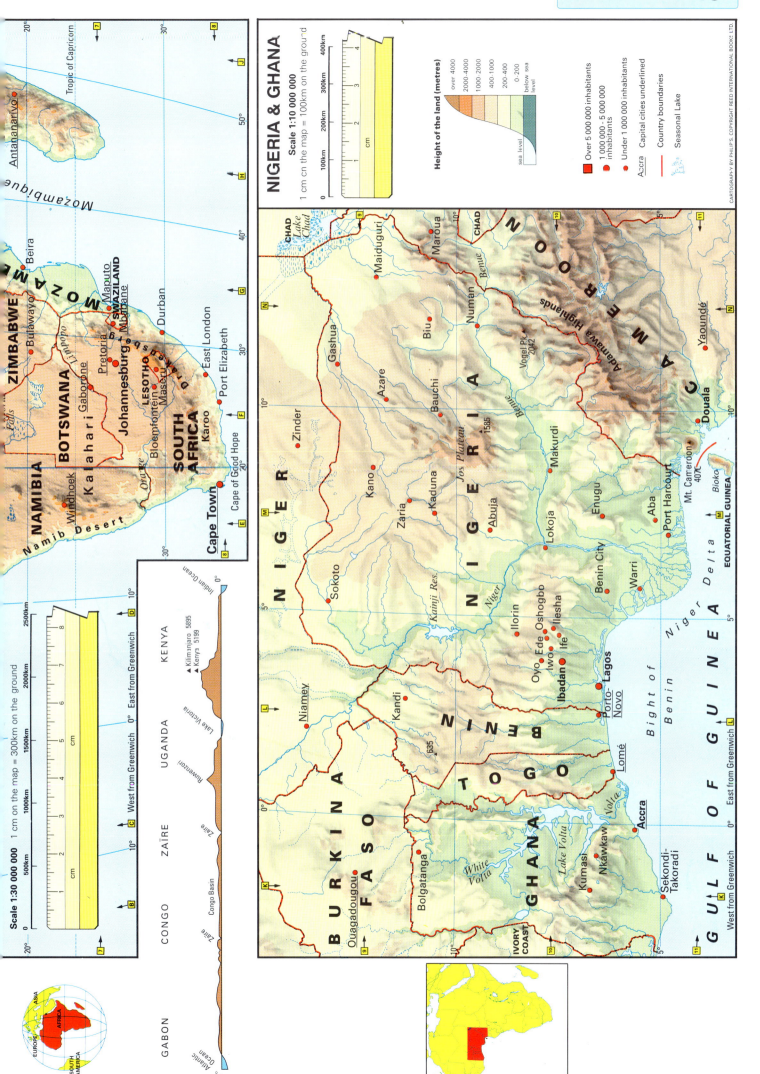

New Zealand
On same scale

COPYRIGHT © GEORGE PHILIP & SON, LTD.

England & Wales
On same scale

SOLOMON ISLANDS

PAPUA NEW GUINEA

Port Moresby

PACIFIC OCEAN

Coral Sea

Chesterfield Is. (France)

Tropic of Capricorn

Great Barrier Reef

C. York
Cape York Peninsula
Torres Strait

Gulf of Carpentaria

C. Arnhem
Arnhem Land

Melville I.

Darwin
Timor Sea
INDONESIA
Sumba
Sumbawa
Timor

INDIAN OCEAN

Kimberley
Ord
Wyndham
Fitzroy

Broome

Port Hedland
Hamersley Range
Great Sandy Desert

WESTERN AUSTRALIA

Gibson Desert

Meekatharra

Carnarvon

Geraldton
Darling Range
Perth
Fremantle
Bunbury
C. Leeuwin
Albany
Esperance

Kalgoorlie-Boulder

Great Victoria Desert

Nullarbor Plain

Great Australian Bight

NORTHERN TERRITORY

Tanami Desert

Tennant Creek
Katherine

Mount Isa

Barkly Tableland

Alice Springs
Macdonnell Ranges

Musgrave Ranges

SOUTH AUSTRALIA

Lake Eyre

L. Torrens
L. Gairdner
Flinders Ranges
Port Augusta
Whyalla
Port Pirie
Port Lincoln
Spencer Gulf
Kangaroo I.

Adelaide
Mount Gambier

QUEENSLAND

Cairns
Townsville

Mackay
Rockhampton
Gladstone
Bundaberg

Brisbane
Gold Coast

Toowoomba
Quilpie
Warrego
Barcoo

Great Dividing Range

NEW SOUTH WALES

Tamworth
Newcastle
Dubbo
Sydney
Wollongong
Canberra
Murrumbidgee
Murray
Darling
Broken Hill
Mildura
Wagga Wagga
Mt. Kosciusko 2230
Australian Alps

VICTORIA
Ballarat
Bendigo
Geelong
Melbourne

Bass Strait
King I.
Flinders I.

TASMANIA
Launceston
Hobart

PACIFIC OCEAN

New Zealand
North Cape
North Island
Auckland
Hamilton
Rotorua
Palmerston North
Wellington
Cook Strait
Tasman Sea
Nelson
South Island
Christchurch
Mt. Cook 3764
Southern Alps
Dunedin
Invercargill
Stewart I.

Scale 1:20 000 000

1 cm on the map = 200 km on the ground

Height of the land (metres)
over 4000
2000–4000
1000–2000
400–1000
200–400
0–200
below sea level
sea level

● Over 5 000 000 inhabitants
● 1 000 000 – 5 000 000 inhabitants
● Under 1 000 000 inhabitants

Canberra Capital cities underlined
Country boundaries
State boundaries
Seasonal lakes

ASIA
NEW ZEALAND
AUSTRALIA
ANTARCTICA

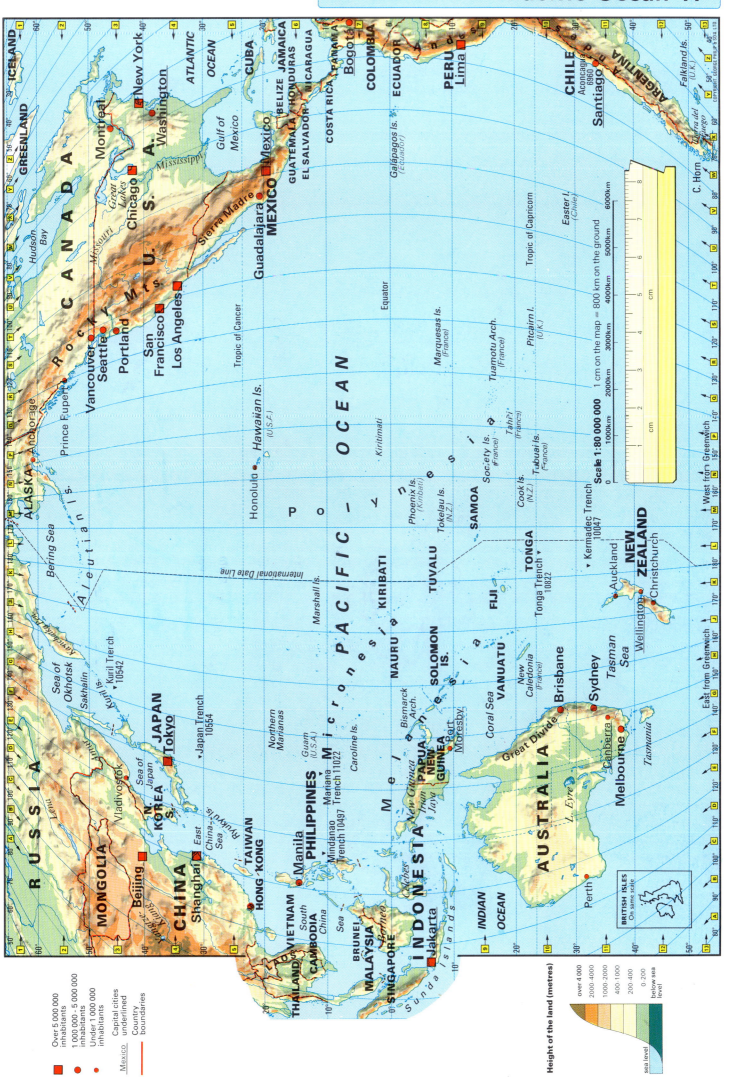

ICELAND

GREENLAND

ATLANTIC OCEAN

CUBA

CANADA

Montreal

Washington

New York

U. S. A.

Chicago

Great Lakes

Gulf of Mexico

JAMAICA

BELIZE

GUATEMALA

HONDURAS

EL SALVADOR

NICARAGUA

COSTA RICA

PANAMA

COLOMBIA

Bogotá

ECUADOR

Andes

PERU

Lima

Hudson Bay

Missouri

Mississippi

Sierra Madre

Guadalajara

MEXICO

Mexico

Rocky Mts.

ALASKA

Anchorage

Prince Rupert

Vancouver

Seattle

Portland

San Francisco

Los Angeles

Tropic of Cancer

Galapagos Is.
(Ecuador)

CHILE

Santiago

Aconcagua
6960

ARGENTINA

PAPUA

Falkland Is.
(U.K.)

COPYRIGHT GEORGE PHILIP & SON LTD.

C. Horn

Tierra del Fuego

Tropic of Capricorn

Easter I.
(Chile)

6000m

5000m

4000m

3000m

2000m

1000km

1 cm on the map = 800 km on the ground

Scale 1:80 000 000

West from Greenwich

PACIFIC – OCEAN

Marquesas Is.
(France)

Tuamotu Arch.
(France)

Pitcairn I.
(U.K.)

Equator

Tahiti
(France)

Society Is.
(France)

Tubuai Is.
(France)

Cook Is.
(N.Z.)

Kermadec Trench
10047

Honolulu

Hawaiian Is.
(U.S.A.)

Kiritimati

Phoenix Is.
(Kiribati)

Tokelau Is.
(N.Z.)

SAMOA

P o l y n e s i a

KIRIBATI

TUVALU

FIJI

TONGA

Tonga Trench
10882

NEW
ZEALAND

Auckland

Wellington

Christchurch

East from Greenwich

NAURU

SOLOMON
IS.

VANUATU

New
Caledonia
(France)

Coral Sea

Brisbane

Sydney

Canberra

Tasman
Sea

Melbourne

Tasmania

Great Divide

L. Eyre

AUSTRALIA

Perth

INDIAN
OCEAN

BRITISH ISLES
On same scale

Northern
Marianas

Guam
(U.S.A.)

Caroline Is.

Mariana
Trench 11022

Mindanao
Trench 10497

Bismarck
Arch.

PAPUA
NEW
GUINEA

Port
Moresby

Irian
Jaya

New Guinea

M e l a n e s i a

M i c r o n e s i a

Marshall Is.

International Date Line

RUSSIA

MONGOLIA

Beijing

CHINA

Shanghai

Amur

Lena

Sea of
Okhotsk

Sakhalin

Kamchatka

Vladivostok

Sea of
Japan

JAPAN

Tokyo

Japan Trench
10554

Kuril Trench
10542

Kuril Is.

Bering Sea

Aleutian Is.

East
China
Sea

TAIWAN

HONG KONG

N. KOREA

S. KOREA

Ryukyu Is.

VIETNAM

LAOS

THAILAND

CAMBODIA

PHILIPPINES

Manila

South
China
Sea

BRUNEI

MALAYSIA

SINGAPORE

INDONESIA

Jakarta

Borneo

Celebes

Sunda Islands

Yangtze

Huang

Height of the land (metres)

over 4 000

2000-4000

1000-2000

400-1000

200-400

0-200

below sea
level

sea level

18 North America

ASIA
RUSSIA
70°
80°
A
180°
2
B
C
160°
D
E
140°
F
G
H
120°
J
K
100°
L
M
80°
N
P
60°
R
S
T
20°
40°
80°
2
70°
3
3
ICELAND

ARCTIC OCEAN

Bering Sea
Bering Strait
C. Barrow
Beaufort Sea
60°
Queen Elizabeth Islands
Magnetic North Pole
Ellesmere I.
GREENLAND (Denmark)
Denmark Strait
60°

Yukon
Brooks Range
ALASKA
Mt. McKinley 6194 (U.S.A.)
Alaska Range
Anchorage
Alaska Peninsula
Mackenzie
Victoria Island
Baffin Bay
Godthåb
Cape Farewell
4
4

Gulf of Alaska
Mt. Logan 6050
Great Bear Lake
Arctic Circle
Baffin Island
Davis Strait
Labrador

50°
BRITISH ISLES On same scale
Queen Charlotte Islands
Coast Mountains
C A N A D A
Great Slave Lake
Hudson Strait
50°

5
Mt. Waddington 4041
Edmonton
Calgary
R O C K Y
Lake Winnipeg
Hudson Bay
St. Lawrence
Quebec
Newfoundland
5

PACIFIC OCEAN
40°
Seattle
Portland
Vancouver
Mt. Rainier 4392
Great Plains
Winnipeg
L. Superior
Lake Winnipeg
Great Lakes
Ottawa
Montreal
Toronto
Boston
New York
40°

6
San Francisco
Sierra Nevada
Snake
Great Salt Lake
Salt Lake City
M o u n t a i n s
Minneapolis
L. Michigan
L. Huron
Detroit
Cleveland
Philadelphia
Baltimore
Washington
ATLANTIC
Bermuda (U.K.)
6

Great Basin
Mt. Whitney 4418
U N I T E D
Denver
Mt. Elbert 4399
Chicago
Pittsburgh
Cincinnati
Appalachian
OCEAN
30°

Los Angeles
Coast Ranges
Death Valley
Colorado
Colorado Plateau
Kansas City
St. Louis
Ohio
30°

Phoenix
Oklahoma
S T A T E S
Memphis
Mississippi
Atlanta
Missouri

Height of the land (metres)

	over 6000
	4000-6000
	2000-4000
	1000-2000
	400-1000
	200-400
sea level	0-200
	below sea level

□ Over 5 000 000 inhabitants
● 1 000 000 - 5 000 000 inhabitants
• Under 1 000 000 inhabitants
Ottawa Capital cities underlined
Country boundaries

San Diego
San Antonio
Lower California
Rio Grande
Houston
Dallas
New Orleans
Gulf of Mexico
Tampa
Florida
Miami
Florida Strait
BAHAMAS
Tropic of Cancer
7

Scale 1:35 000 000   1 cm on the map = 350 km on the ground

Sierra Madre
Monterrey
MEXICO
Gulf of California
CUBA
Havana
HAITI
DOM. REP.
20°

8
Guadalajara
Revilla Gigedo Is. (Mexico)
Mexico City
BELIZE
JAMAICA
Caribbean Sea
8

0 500km 1000km 1500km 2000km 2500km

9
1 cm 2 3 4 5 6 7 8 cm
GUATEMALA
Guatemala
EL SALVADOR
HONDURAS
NICARAGUA
COSTA RICA
PANAMA
SOUTH AMERICA
VENEZUELA
COLOMBIA
9

130°
G
120°
H
110° West from Greenwich
J
100°
K
90°
L
80°
M
70°
COPYRIGHT. GEORGE PHILIP & SON LTD.

Cross section

ASIA EUROPE AFRICA NORTH AMERICA SOUTH AMERICA

Pacific Ocean
Mt. Shasta 4317
Sierra Nevada
Wasatch Mts.
Colorado
Mt. Elbert 4399
Rocky Mts.
Great Plains
Missouri
Mississippi
Ohio
Allegheny Mts.
Appalachian Mts.
Atlantic Ocean
40°N   40°N

West from Greenwich 100°

COPYRIGHT GEORGE PHILIP & SON, LTD.

BRITISH ISLES
On same scale

Height of the land (metres)

over 6000	
4000-6000	
2000-4000	
1000-2000	
400-1000	
200-400	
0-200	
sea level	
below sea level	

◼ Over 5 000 000 inhabitants
● 1 000 000 – 5 000 000 inhabitants
• Under 1 000 000 inhabitants
Lima Capital cities underlined
— Country boundaries

Scale 1:35 000 000   1 cm on the map = 350 km on the ground

0   500km   1000km   1500km   2000km   2500km

Cross section

NORTH AMERICA   SOUTH AMERICA   AFRICA   ANTARCTICA

CHILE   BOLIVIA   PARAGUAY   BRAZIL

▲ Ojos del Salado 6863
▲ Ancohuma & Illampu 6550

Pacific Ocean Andes Picomayo Gran Chaco Paraguay Verde Paraná Brazilian Highlands São Francisco Doce Atlantic Ocean

20° S   20° S

Height of the land (metres)

over 4000	
2000-4000	
1000-2000	
400-1000	
200-400	
0-200	
sea level	below sea level

■ Over 5 000 000 inhabitants

● 1 000 000 - 5 000 000 inhabitants

● Under 1 000 000 inhabitants

<u>Ottawa</u> Capital cities underlined

—— Country boundaries

—— State boundaries

CONN. = Connecticut
DEL. = Delaware
MASS. = Massachusetts
R.I. = Rhode Island

Hawaii
Scale 1:10 000 000
0   100km   200km

A B C D E F G

San Diego
Phoenix
Tucson
Ciudad Juarez
Hermosillo
Chihuahua
Culiacan
Durango
Monterrey
Aguascalientes
Guadalajara
Mexico
Popocatepetl 5452 Citlaltepetl 5700
Puebla
Acapulco
Mérida
Belmopan
BELIZE
GUATEMALA
Guatemala 4217
San Pedro S
HONDURAS
San Salvador
Tegucigal
EL SALVADOR
NICARA
Managua
CO

Dallas
Houston
New Orleans
Birmingham
Corpus Christi
Tampico

UNITED STATE

Gulf of California
Lower California
Gulf of Mexico
Gulf of Campeche
Yucatan
Gulf of Honduras
Gulf of Tehuantepec
Isthmus of Tehuantepec

Sierra Madre
Rio Grande
Rio Grande de Santiago
Colorado
Sonora
Mississippi
Alabama
Mississippi Delta

C. San Lucas
Las Tres Marías
C. Corrientes
Revilla Gigedo Is.

2896
3150
4054
3353

Tropic of Cancer

PACIFIC

OCEAN

30°
25°
20°
15°
10°
5°

115° 110° 105° 100° 95° 90°

West from Greenwich

ENGLAND & WALES
On same scale

CARTOGRAPHY BY PHILIP'S. COPYRIGHT REED INTERNATIONAL BOOKS

Height of the land (metres)

over 4000
2000-4000
1000-2000
400-1000
200-400
0-200
sea level
below sea level

■ Over 5 000 000 inhabitants

● 1 000 000 - 5 000 000 inhabitants

• Under 1 000 000 inhabitants

<u>Mexico</u> Capital cities underlined

——— Country boundaries

tlanta

C. Fear

ATLANTIC OCEAN

Bermuda
Hamilton

Jacksonville

Florida

Grand
Bahama I.

Miami

C. Sable

Florida Str.

Nassau

BAHAMAS

Tropic of Cancer

avana

C U B A

Turks &
Caicos Is.

2000

Santiago
de Cuba

JAMAICA

Windward Passage

Santiago

HAITI 3175

**DOMINICAN
REP.**

Mona Passage

San Juan

▲1338

Virgin Is.

**ANTIGUA &
BARBUDA**

St. John's

Port au Prince

2280

Santo
Domingo

Puerto Rico

**ST. KITTS-
NEVIS**

Kingston

Grand
Cayman

Guadeloupe

Pointe à Pitre

DOMINICA

Leeward
Islands

Fort de France

Martinique

ST. LUCIA

C a r i b b e a n   S e a

Windward Islands

BARBADOS

Bridgetown

**ST. VINCENT &
THE GRENADINES**

Gulf of Venezuela

Aruba

GRENADA

Tobago

Port of Spain

**TRINIDAD &
TOBAGO**

**NETH.
ANTILLES**

Barranquilla

Cartagena

▲5800

Sierra Nevada
de Santa Marta

Maracaibo

Caracas

Barquisimeto

Delta of the
Orinoco

G. of
Darién

Orinoco

Ciudad Bolívar

Georgetown

RICA

San José

Panama

▲3374

P A N A M A

Gulf of
Panama

5007 ▲

Cord. de Mérida

4100 ▲

V E N E Z U E L A

▲ 2285

G U Y A N A

▲ 2560

Roraima 2810

SURINAM

Medellín

C O L O M B I A

Sierra Pacaraima

Essequibo

1280

5215 ▲
Tolima

Bogotá

Cali

Guaviare

B R A Z I L

▲ 4646

West from Greenwich

Scale 1:15 000 000   1 cm on the map = 150km on the ground

0   300km   600km   900km   1200km   1500km

1   2   3   4   5   6   7   8   9   10

cm   cm   cm

Scale 1:50 000 000   1 cm on the map = 500 km on the ground

0   500km 1000km 1500km 2000km 2500km 3000km

Height of the land (metres)

over 4000
2000-4000
1000-2000
400-1000
200-400
0-200
sea level
below sea level

☐ Over 5 000 000 inhabitants

● 1 000 000 - 5 000 000 inhabitants

• Under 1 000 000 inhabitants

Oslo   Capital cities underlined

○ Davis   Research station and the country which runs it

〰 Limit of permanently frozen sea

◇ Icebergs

⋯ Furthest extent of Icebergs

☐ Land permanently covered with ice

—100— Height of ice (in metres)

COPYRIGHT. GEORGE PHILIP & SON. LTD.

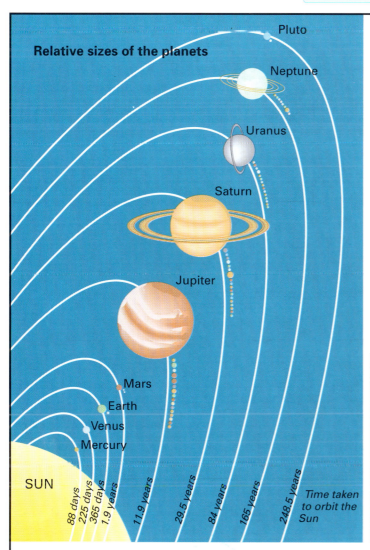

Relative sizes of the planets

Pluto
Neptune
Uranus
Saturn
Jupiter
Mars
Earth
Venus
Mercury
SUN

88 days
225 days
365 days
1.9 years
11.9 years
29.5 years
84 years
165 years
248.5 years

Time taken to orbit the Sun

THE SOLAR SYSTEM

The universe is made up of many galaxies, or collection of stars. Our galaxy is called the Milky Way. It is made up of about 100 000 stars. The Sun is one of these stars. Nine planets revolve round the Sun. The Earth is one of these planets. The Sun, its' planets and their satellites are known as the Solar System.

The Sun is the only source of light and heat in the Solar System. The other planets are visible from the Earth because of the sunlight which they reflect. The planets move in two ways at once. They revolve round, or orbit the Sun in an anti-clockwise direction, each planet keeping a fixed distance from the Sun. They also rotate anti-clockwise on their own axes.

THE PLANETS

The diagram on the left shows the time each planet takes to orbit the Sun.

	Time taken to rotate	Distance from the Sun (km)	Equatorial Diameter (km)
MERCURY	59 days	58 000 000	4 878
VENUS	243 days	108 000 000	12 104
EARTH	24 hours	150 000 000	12 756
MARS	25 hours	228 000 000	6 794
JUPITER	10 hours	778 000 000	142 800
SATURN	10 hours	1 427 000 000	120 000
URANUS	17 hours	2 870 000 000	52 000
NEPTUNE	16 hours	4 497 000 000	48 400
PLUTO	6 days	5 900 000 000	3 000

THE EARTH

The Earth travels at a speed of over 107 000 kilometres an hour and rotates once in 24 hours. Places on the equator are spinning at 1660 kilometres an hour. We have day and night and different seasons because of the way the Earth spins, see page 40.

PHYSICAL DIMENSIONS

Surface area of the Earth	510 000 000 km²
Land surface	149 000 000 km²
Water surface	361 000 000 km²
Polar diameter	12 713.8 km
Polar circumference	40 009 km
Polar radius	6 356.9 km
Equatorial diameter	12 756.8 km
Equatorial circumference	40 077 km
Equatorial radius	6 378.4 km
Volume of the Earth	1 083 230 x 10⁶ km³
Mass of the Earth	5.9 x 10²¹ tonnes
Distance to Sun	150 000 000 km
Distance to Moon	384 400 km
Depth of atmosphere	175 km
Main gases in the atmosphere	nitrogen (78%) oxygen (21%)

Height of the land (metres)

over 4000
2000-4000
1000-2000
400-1000
200-400
0-200
sea level
below sea level

Projection: Hammers Equal Area

Continent	Area, '000 km²	Coldest place, °C		Hottest place, °C		Wettest place (average annual rainfall, mm)		(average annual rainfall, mm)
Asia	44 500	Verkhoyansk, Russia -68°C	1	Tirat Zevi, Israel 54°C	8	Cherrapunji, India 11 430	15	Aden, Yemen 46
Africa	30 302	Ifrane, Morocco -24°C	2	El Azizia, Libya 58°C	9	Debundscha, Cameroon 10 290	16	Wadi Halfa, Sudan 2
North America	24 241	Snag, Yukon -63°C	3	Death Valley, California 57°C	10	Henderson Lake, Canada 6 500	17	Bataques, Mexico 30
South America	17 793	Sarmiento, Argentina -33°C	4	Rivadavia, Argentina 49°C	11	Quibdó, Colombia 8 990	18	Arica, Chile 0.8
Antarctica	14 000	Vostok -89°C	5	Vanda Station 15°C	12			
Europe	9 957	Ust'Shchugor, Russia -55°C	6	Seville, Spain 50°C	13	Crkvice, Yugoslavia 4 650	19	Astrakhan, Russia 160
Oceania	8 557	Charlotte Pass, Australia -22°C	7	Cloncurry, Australia 53°C	14	Tully, Australia 4 550	20	Muika, Australia 100

Scale 1:80 000 000
1 cm on the map = 800 km on the ground

— Continental boundaries

World - largest seas, '000 km²		World - largest lakes, '000 km²		World - longest rivers, km	
cific Ocean 165 721	(27)	Caspian Sea 424	(37)	Nile 6 690	(47)
antic Ocean 81 660	(28)	Lake Superior 82	(38)	Amazon 6 280	(48)
ian Ocean 73 442	(29)	Lake Victoria 69	(39)	Mississippi-Missouri 6 270	(49)
ctic Ocean 14 351	(30)	Lake Huron 60	(40)	Yangtze-Kiang 4 990	(50)
diterranean Sea 2 966	(31)	Lake Michigan 58	(41)	Zaïre 4 670	(51)
uth China Sea 2 318	(32)	Aral Sea 36	(42)	Amur 4 410	(52)
ring Sea 2 274	(33)	Lake Tanganyika 33	(43)	Hwang-Ho 4 350	(53)
ribbean Sea 1 942	(34)	Lake Baikal 31	(44)	Lena 4 260	(54)
lf of Mexico 1 813	(35)	Great Bear Lake 31	(45)	Mekong 4 180	(55)
a of Okhotsk 1 528	(36)	Lake Malawi 31	(46)	Niger 4 180	(56)

World - largest islands, '000 km²		World - highest peaks, m		World - deepest trenches, m	
Greenland 2 176	(57)	Himalayas: Mt. Everest 8 848	(67)	Mariana Trench 11 022	(77)
New Guinea 777	(58)	Karakoram Ra: K2 8 611	(68)	Tonga Trench 10 822	(78)
Borneo 725	(59)	Pamirs: Communism Pk. 7 495	(69)	Japan Trench 10 554	(79)
Madagascar 590	(60)	Tian Shan: Pik Pobedy 7 444	(70)	Kuril Trench 10 542	(80)
Baffin Island 476	(61)	Andes: Aconcagua 6 960	(71)	Mindanao Trench 10 497	(81)
Sumatra 474	(62)	Rocky Mts: Mt. McKinley 6 194	(72)	Kermadec Trench 10 047	(82)
Honshu 228	(63)	East Africa: Mt. Kilimanjaro 5 895	(73)	Milwaukee Deep 9 200	(83)
Great Britain 217	(64)	Caucasus: Elbrus 5 633	(74)	Bougainville Trench 9 140	(84)
Victoria Island 212	(65)	Antarctica: Vinson Massif 5 139	(75)	South Sandwich Island Trench 8 428	(85)
Ellesmere Island 197	(66)	Alps: Mt. Blanc 4 810	(76)	Aleutian Trench 7 822	(86)

Projection: Hammers Equal Area

Country	Population in thousands 1995 estimate	Area in thous' km²	Country	Population in thousands 1995 estimate	Area in thous' km²	Country	Population in thousands 1995 estimate	Area in thous' km²	Country	Population in thousands 1995 estimate	Area in thous' km²	Country	Population in thousands 1995 estimate
China	1 226 944	9 597	Nigeria	88 515	924	Italy	57 181	301	Argentina	34 663	2 767	Uzbekistan	22 833
India	942 989	3 288	Germany	82 000	357	Ukraine	52 027	604	Sudan	29 980	2 506	Nepal	21 953
United States	263 563	9 373	Vietnam	74 580	332	Ethiopia	51 600	1 128	Canada	29 972	9 976	Venezuela	21 810
Indonesia	198 644	1 905	Iran	68 885	1 648	Burma	46 580	677	Tanzania	29 710	945	Uganda	21 466
Brazil	161 416	8 512	Philippines	67 167	300	South Korea	45 088	99	Kenya	28 240	580	Taiwan	21 100
Russia	148 385	17 075	Egypt	64 100	1 001	Zaïre	44 504	2 345	Algeria	27 936	2 382	Iraq	20 184
Pakistan	143 595	796	Turkey	61 303	779	South Africa	44 000	1 220	Morocco	26 857	447	Malaysia	20 174
Japan	125 156	378	Thailand	58 432	513	Spain	39 664	505	North Korea	23 931	121	Afghanistan	19 509
Bangladesh	118 342	144	United Kingdom	58 306	243	Poland	38 587	313	Peru	23 588	1 285	Saudi Arabia	18 395
Mexico	93 342	1 958	France	58 286	552	Colombia	34 948	1 139	Romania	22 863	238	Sri Lanka	18 359

Scale 1:80 000 000
1 cm on the map = 800 km on the ground

Scale 1:80 000 000

Country	Population in thousands 1995 estimate	Area in thous' km²	Country	Population in thousands 1995 estimate	Area in thous' km²	Country	Population in thousands 1995 estimate	Area in thous' km²	Country	Population in thousands 1995 estimate	Area in thous' km²	Country	Population in thousands 1995 estimate	Area in thous' km²	Country	Population in thousands 1995 estimate	Area in thous' km²
Australia	18 107	7 687	Cameroon	13 232	475	Belarus	10 500	208	Tunisia	8 906	164	Haiti	7 180	28
...zambique	17 800	802	Zimbabwe	11 453	391	Czech Republic	10 500	79	Sweden	8 893	450	Guinea	6 702	246
...ana	17 462	239	Ecuador	11 384	284	Hungary	10 500	93	Bulgaria	8 771	111	Burundi	6 412	28
...akstan	17 099	2 717	Cuba	11 050	111	Cambodia	10 452	181	Senegal	8 308	197	Chad	6 314	1 284
...herlands	15 495	42	Yugoslavia	10 881	102	Burkina Faso	10 326	274	Austria	8 004	84	Tajikistan	6 102	143
...dagascar	15 206	587	Angola	10 844	1 247	Belgium	10 140	31	Bolivia	7 900	1 099	Hong Kong	6 000	1
...ia	14 614	185	Mali	10 700	1 240	Malawi	9 800	118	Rwanda	7 899	26	Honduras	5 940	112
...nen	14 609	528	Guatemala	10 624	109	Zambia	9 500	753	Dominican Rep.	7 818	49	El Salvador	5 743	21
...le	14 271	757	Portugal	10 600	92	Somalia	9 180	638	Azerbaijan	7 559	87	Israel	5 696	27
...ry Coast	14 271	322	Greece	10 510	132	Niger	9 149	1 267	Switzerland	7 268	41	Jordan	5 547	89

CLIMATE REGIONS

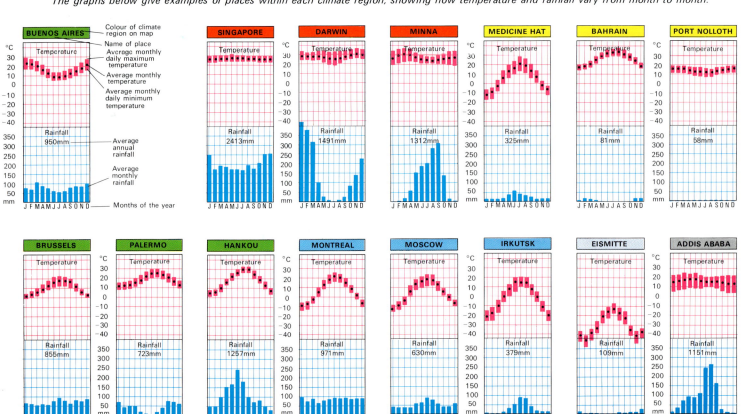

	Tropical climate *(hot and wet)*		Mild climate *(warm and wet)*		Polar climate *(very cold and dry)*
	Dry climate *(desert and steppe)*		Continental climate *(cold and wet)*		Mountainous areas where altitude affects climate type

The map shows how the world can be divided into 6 broad climate regions.

CLIMATE GRAPHS

The graphs below give examples of places within each climate region, showing how temperature and rainfall vary from month to month.

JANUARY TEMPERATURE

Winter in the northern hemisphere

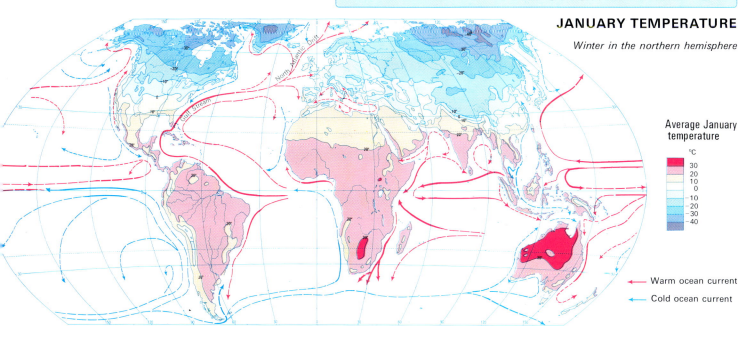

Average January
temperature

°C

30
20
10
0
−10
−20
−30
−40

→ Warm ocean current

→ Cold ocean current

JULY TEMPERATURE

Summer in the northern hemisphere

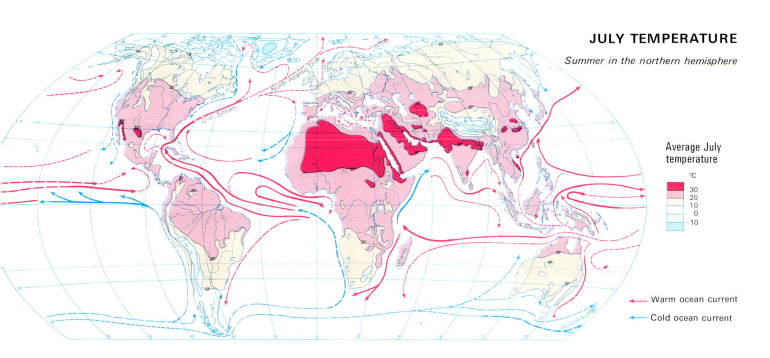

Average July
temperature

°C

30
20
10
0
−10

→ Warm ocean current

→ Cold ocean current

YEARLY RAINFALL

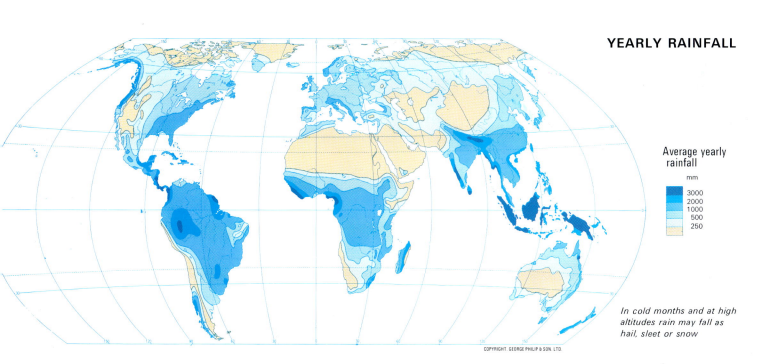

Average yearly
rainfall

mm

3000
2000
1000
500
250

*In cold months and at high
altitudes rain may fall as
hail, sleet or snow*

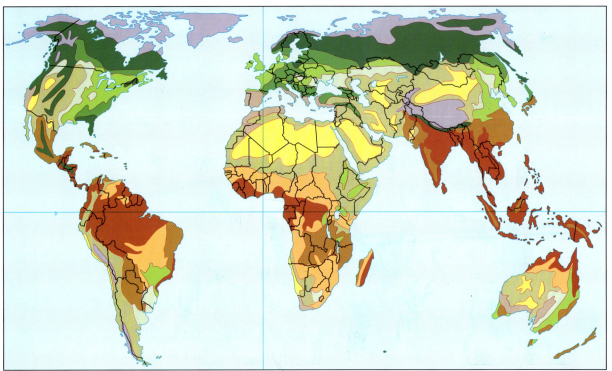

NATURAL VEGETATION

The map shows the type of vegetation that would grow if people were not there. People have cleared forests and natural grasslands for thousands of years. Most of the broadleaf deciduous woodland that would naturally cover the British Isles has been cleared for farming and for building. In more recent years, much of the tropical broadleaf rainforest and monsoon forests have been felled.

Tundra and mountain vegetation	
Needleleaf evergreen forest	
Mixed forest of needleleaf evergreen and broadleaf deciduous trees	
Broadleaf deciduous woodland	
Mid-latitude grassland	
Evergreen broadleaf and deciduous trees, shrubs and herbs	
Semi-desert scrub	
Desert	
Tropical grassland (savanna)	
Tropical broadleaf rainforest and needleleaf forest	
Sub-tropical broadleaf and needleleaf forest	

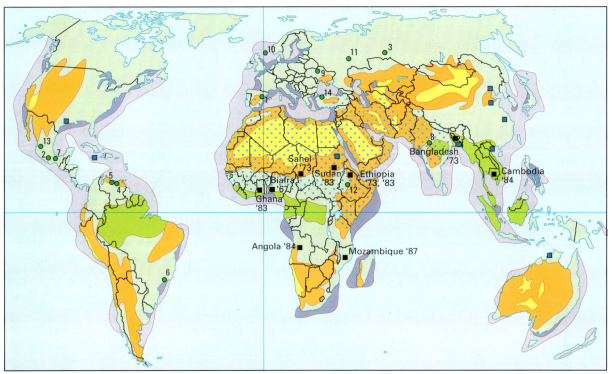

NATURAL DISASTERS

Locust invasion are	
■ Major famines	
■ Major storms and floo	

ENVIRONMENTAL CONCERNS

● Selected recent industrial accidents causing deaths

	Heavily polluted seas and lakes
	Other polluted seas and lakes
	Areas where the forest is being rapidly cut down (deforestation)
	Areas of continuous drought (deserts)
	Areas which are turning into desert due to soil erosion plus low rainfall (desertification)

No. ON MAP	DATE	LOCATION	CAUSE	No. OF DEATHS
1.	1978	Los Alfaques, Spain	Gas explosion	216
2.	1978	Xilatopec, Mexico	Gas explosion	100
3.	1979	Novosibirsk, Russia	Chemical plant accident	300
4.	1981	Tacoa, Venezuela	Oil explosion	145
5.	1982	Caracas, Venezuela	Explosives accident	101
6.	1984	São Paulo, Brazil	Gas explosion	508
7.	1984	Ixhuatepec, Mexico	Gas explosion	452
8.	1984	Bhopal, India	Chemical leakage	2500
9.	1986	Chernobyl, Ukraine	Nuclear reactor explosion	31
10.	1988	Piper Alpha, North Sea	Gas explosion	166
11.	1989	Ufa, Russia	Gas explosion	650
12.	1991	Addis Ababa, Ethiopia	Explosives accident	100
13.	1992	Guadalajara, Mexico	Gas explosion	206
14.	1992	Kozlu, Turkey	Gas explosion	272

VOLCANOES

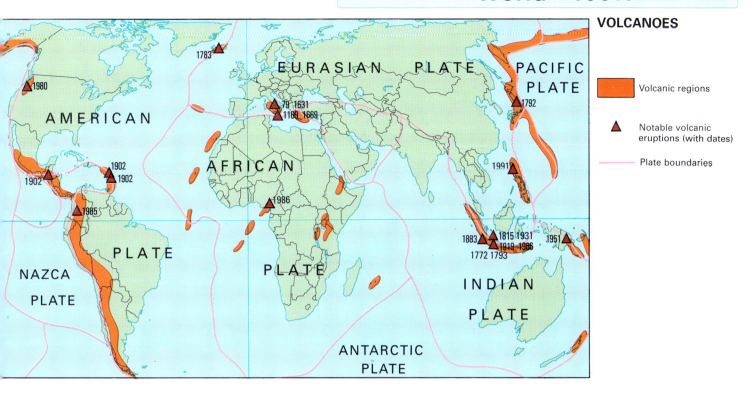

Volcanic regions

▲ **Notable volcanic eruptions (with dates)**

— **Plate boundaries**

Labels on map: EURASIAN PLATE, PACIFIC PLATE, AMERICAN PLATE, AFRICAN PLATE, NAZCA PLATE, PLATE, INDIAN PLATE, ANTARCTIC PLATE

Dates on map: 1783, 1980, 1902, 1902, 1902, 1985, 79 1631, 1169 1669, 1986, 1792, 1991, 1883, 1815 1931, 1919 1966, 1772 1793, 1951

TABLE VOLCANOES

Volcano	Deaths
Vesuvius, Italy	16,000
Mount Etna, Sicily	20,000
Papandajan, Java	3,000
Skaptar Jökull, Iceland	10,000

Year	Volcano	Deaths
1792	Unzen-Dake, Japan	15,000
1793	Miyi-Yama, Indonesia	50,000
1815	Tambora, Java	12,000
1883	Krakatoa, Indonesia	50,000
1902	Soufrière, St. Vincent	3,000
1902	Mount Pelée, Martinique	40,000
1902	Santa Maria, Guatemala	6,000
1911	Mount Taal, Philippines	1,400

Year	Volcano	Deaths
1931	Merapi, Java	1,000
1951	Mount Lamington, Papua New Guinea	6,000
1966	Mount Kelud, Java	1,000
1980	Mount St. Helens, USA	100
1985	Nevado del Ruiz, Colombia	22,940
1986	Wum, Cameroon	1,700
1991	Mount Pinatubo, Philippines	300
1993	Mount Mayon, Philippines	77

EARTHQUAKES

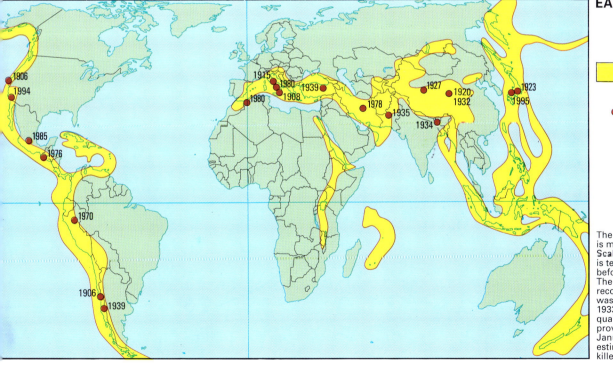

Earthquake regions

● **Notable earthquakes (with dates)**

Dates on map: 1906, 1994, 1985, 1976, 1970, 1906, 1939, 1915, 1980, 1939, 1980, 1908, 1978, 1935, 1934, 1927, 1920, 1932, 1923, 1995

The magnitude of an earthquake is measured on the Richter Scale. Each level of magnitude is ten times greater than the one before.
The highest magnitude recorded on the Richter Scale was 8.9 in Japan on 2 March 1933. The most devastating quake ever was in Shaanxi province, Central China, on 24 January 1566 when an estimated 830 000 people were killed.

NOTABLE EARTHQUAKES SINCE 1900

Location	Mag.	Deaths
San Francisco, USA	8.3	503
Valparaiso, Chile	8.6	22,000
Messina, Italy	7.5	83,000
Avezzano, Italy	7.5	30,000
Gansu (Kansu), China	8.6	180,000
Yokohama, Japan	8.3	143,000
Nan Shan, China	8.3	200,000
Gansu (Kansu), China	7.6	70,000
Bihar, India/ Nepal	8.4	10,700

Year	Location	Mag.	Deaths
1935	Quetta, India*	7.5	60,000
1939	Chillan, Chile	8.3	28,000
1939	Erzincan, Turkey	7.9	30,000
1960	Agadir, Morocco	5.8	12,000
1962	Khorasan, Iran	7.1	12,230
1963	Skopje, Yugoslavia**	6.0	1,000
1964	Anchorage, Alaska	8.4	131
1968	N.E.Iran	7.4	12,000
1970	N. Peru	7.7	66,794
1972	Managua, Nicaragua	6.2	5,000
1974	N. Pakistan	6.3	5,200
1976	Guatemala	7.5	22,778
1976	Tangshan, China	8.2	650,000

Year	Location	Mag.	Deaths
1978	Tabas, Iran	7.7	25,000
1980	El Asnam, Algeria	7.3	20,000
1980	S. Italy	7.2	4,800
1985	Mexico City, Mexico	8.1	4,200
1988	N.W. Armenia	6.8	55,000
1990	N. Iran	7.7	36,000
1993	Maharashtra, India	6.4	30,000
1994	Los Angeles, USA	6.6	57
1995	Kōbe, Japan	7.2	5,000

*now Pakistan

**now Macedonia

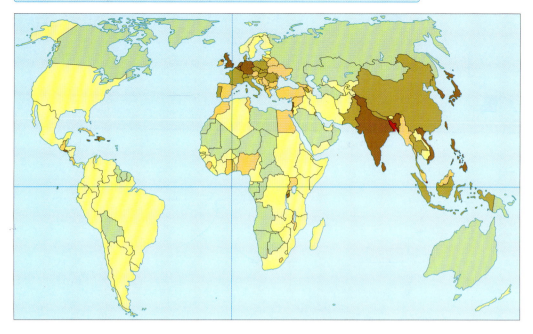

POPULATION DENSITY BY COUNTRY

Number of people per square kilometre in 1991

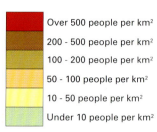

■ (red)	Over 500 people per km²
■ (dark brown)	200 - 500 people per km²
■ (olive)	100 - 200 people per km²
■ (tan)	50 - 100 people per km²
■ (yellow)	10 - 50 people per km²
■ (pale green)	Under 10 people per km²

Top 5 countries		Bottom 5 countries	
Macau	24 850 per km²	Mauritania	2.0 per km²
Hong Kong	5 960 per km²	Mongolia	1.5 per km²
Singapore	4 667 per km²	French Guiana	1.1 per km²
Gibraltar	3 000 per km²	Congo	0.7 per km²
Malta	1 333 per km²	Greenland	0.2 per km²

U.K. 238 per km²

POPULATION CHANGE 1990-2000

The predicted population change for the years 1990-2000

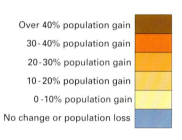

■ (dark brown)	Over 40% population gain
■ (orange)	30 - 40% population gain
■ (light orange)	20 - 30% population gain
■ (pale orange)	10 - 20% population gain
■ (pale yellow)	0 - 10% population gain
■ (blue)	No change or population loss

Top 5 countries		Bottom 5 countries	
Kuwait	+75.9%	Belgium	-0.1%
Namibia	+62.5%	Hungary	-0.2%
Afghanistan	+60.1%	Grenada	-2.4%
Mali	+55.5%	Germany	-3.2%
Tanzania	+54.6%	Tonga	-3.2%

U.K. +2.0%

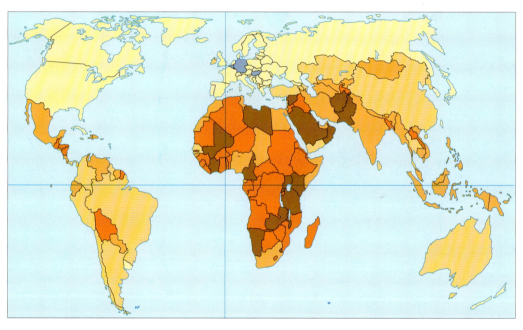

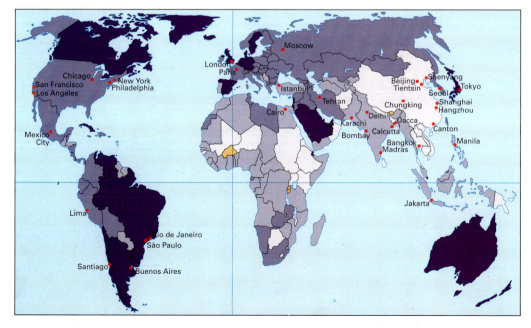

URBAN POPULATION

Percentage of total population living in towns and cities 1990

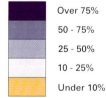

■ (very dark)	Over 75%
■ (dark grey-blue)	50 - 75%
■ (grey)	25 - 50%
■ (white)	10 - 25%
■ (orange)	Under 10%

• Cities with over 5 000 000 inhabitants

New York	18 087 000	Tokyo	11 936 000
Los Angeles	14 532 000	Buenos Aires	11 256 000
Mexico City	13 636 000	Calcutta	10 916 000
Bombay	12 572 000	Seoul	10 628 000
Shanghai	12 320 000	São Paulo	9 627 000

POPULATION BY CONTINENTS

In this diagram the size of each continent is in proportion to its population. Each square represents 1% of the projected world population of 5 720 651 000 in 1995.

Top 20 countries (thousands)	
China	1 208 841
India	918 570
U.S.A.	260 631
Indonesia	194 615
Brazil	159 143
Russia	147 370
Pakistan	136 645
Japan	124 815
Bangladesh	117 787
Mexico	91 858
Nigeria	88 515
Germany	80 278
Vietnam	72 931
Philippines	66 188
Iran	65 758
Egypt	61 636
Turkey	60 771
Thailand	58 183
U.K.	58 091
France	57 747

NORTH AMERICA

EUROPE

ASIA

AFRICA

SOUTH AMERICA

OCEANIA

LIFE EXPECTANCY

The average number of years a person born between 1990-95 can be expected to live

Over 75 years
70 - 75 years
65 - 70 years
60 - 65 years
55 - 60 years
50 - 55 years
Under 50 years

Highest life expectancy		Lowest life expectancy	
Japan	79 years	Gambia	45 years
Iceland	78 years	Guinea	45 years
Sweden	78 years	Afghanistan	44 years
Hong Kong	78 years	Guinea-Bissau	44 years
Switzerland	78 years	Sierra Leone	43 years
	U.K.	76 years	

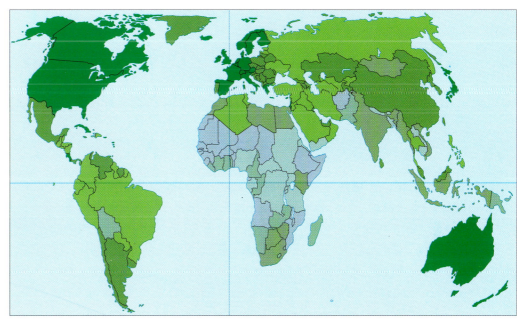

FAMILY SIZE

The average number of children born to each woman during her lifetime

6 children or more
5 children or more
4 children or more
3 children or more
2 children or more
1 child or more

In the U.K. the average family size is 1.8 children per family, whilst in Kenya the average size is 6.8 children.

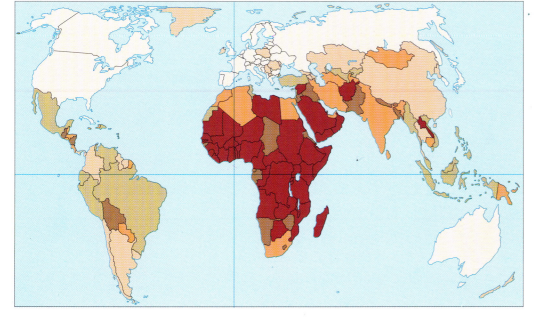

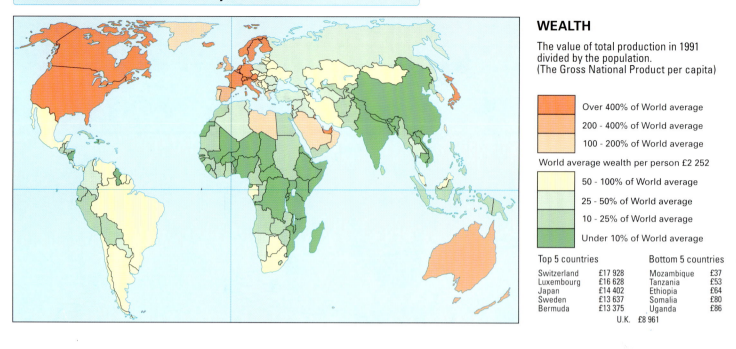

WEALTH

The value of total production in 1991 divided by the population. (The Gross National Product per capita)

- Over 400% of World average
- 200 - 400% of World average
- 100 - 200% of World average

World average wealth per person £2 252

- 50 - 100% of World average
- 25 - 50% of World average
- 10 - 25% of World average
- Under 10% of World average

Top 5 countries		Bottom 5 countries	
Switzerland	£17 928	Mozambique	£37
Luxembourg	£16 628	Tanzania	£53
Japan	£14 402	Ethiopia	£64
Sweden	£13 637	Somalia	£80
Bermuda	£13 375	Uganda	£86
		U.K.	£8 961

WATER SUPPLY

Percentage of total population with access to safe drinking water (latest available year)

- Over 90% with safe water
- 75 - 90% with safe water
- 60 - 75% with safe water
- 45 - 60% with safe water
- 30 - 45% with safe water
- Under 30% with safe water

Least well provided countries

Mozambique	22%	Afghanistan	29%
Madagascar	23%	Burma	32%
Central African Rep.	24%	Papua New Guinea	33%
Vietnam	24%	Uganda	33%
Ethiopia	25%	Bhutan	34%

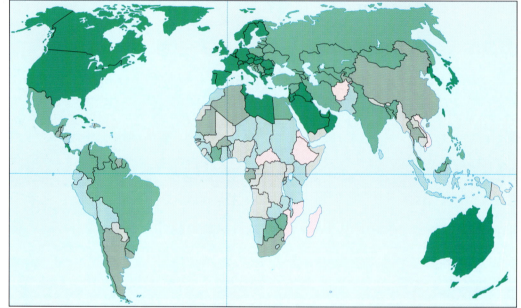

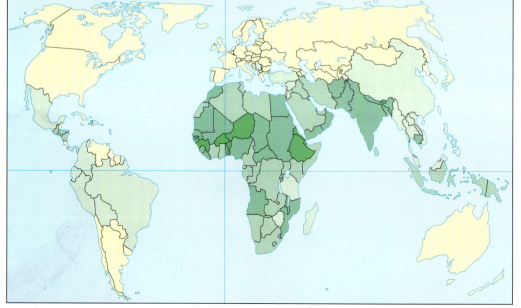

ILLITERACY

Percentage of the total population unable to read or write (latest available year)

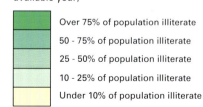

- Over 75% of population illiterate
- 50 - 75% of population illiterate
- 25 - 50% of population illiterate
- 10 - 25% of population illiterate
- Under 10% of population illiterate

Educational expenditure per person (latest available year)

Top 5 countries		Bottom 5 countries	
Sweden	£551	Chad	£1
Qatar	£547	Bangladesh	£2
Canada	£544	Ethiopia	£2
Norway	£537	Nepal	£2
Switzerland	£440	Somalia	£2
		U.K.	£247

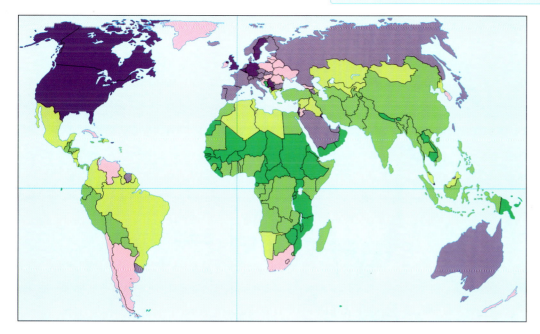

EMPLOYMENT

The ratio of the industrial workforce to the agricultural workforce

This map shows the number of industrial workers in each country for every 100 agricultural workers

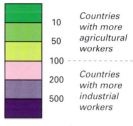

10	Countries with more agricultural workers
50	
100	
200	Countries with more industrial workers
500	

DAILY FOOD CONSUMPTION

The average daily amount of food each person eats, measured in Kilocalories, latest available year

Over 3 500 K. cal per person

3 000 - 3 500 K. cal per person

2 500 - 3 000 K. cal per person

2 000 - 2 500 K. cal per person

Under 2 000 K. cal per person

No available data

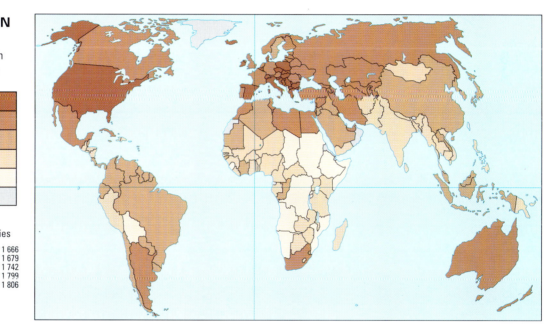

Top 5 countries		Bottom 5 countries	
Belgium	3 902	Ethiopia	1 666
Greece	3 825	Mozambique	1 679
Ireland	3 778	Chad	1 742
Bulgaria	3 707	Sierra Leone	1 799
U.S.A.	3 670	Angola	1 806
	U.K.	3 148	

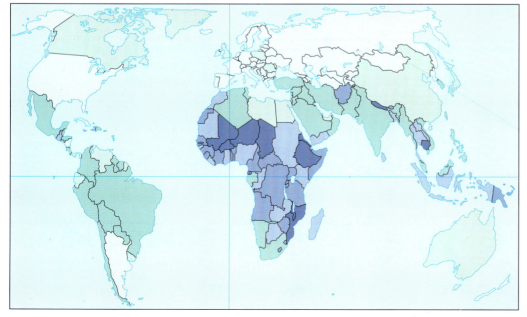

HEALTH CARE

Number of people per doctor, latest available year

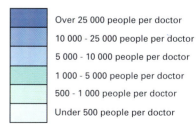

Over 25 000 people per doctor

10 000 - 25 000 people per doctor

5 000 - 10 000 people per doctor

1 000 - 5 000 people per doctor

500 - 1 000 people per doctor

Under 500 people per doctor

Most people per doctor		Least people per doctor	
Ethiopia	78 740	Russia	235
Equatorial Guinea	62 000	Austria	256
Mozambique	50 817	Hungary	304
Chad	47 640	Spain	316
Burkina Faso	42 128	Belgium	342
	U.K.	668	

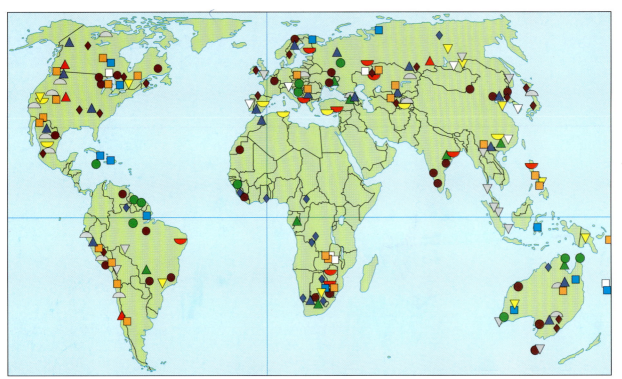

MINERALS

▽ **Gold**

World total (1991)
1,782 tonnes

South Africa	33.7%
U.S.A.	16.8%
Former U.S.S.R.	13.6%
Australia	13.1%
Canada	9.9%

◗ **Silver**

World total (1991)
14,241 tonnes

Mexico	16.1%
U.S.A.	13.0%
Peru	12.4%
Canada	9.4%
Former U.S.S.R.	8.9%

◆ **Diamonds**

World total (1991)
99,200,000 carats

Australia	36.3%
Zaïre	19.2%
Botswana	16.6%
Former U.S.S.R.	13.1%
South Africa	8.3%

● **Iron Ore**

World total (1991)
946,000,000 tonnes

Former U.S.S.R.	20.9%
China	18.6%
Brazil	15.9%
Australia	12.9%
U.S.A.	5.9%

■ **Copper**

World total (1991)
9,112,000 tonnes

Chile	20.0%
U.S.A.	17.9%
Former U.S.S.R.	9.2%
Canada	8.8%
Zambia	4.6%

■ **Nickel**

World total (1991)
871,000 tonnes

Former U.S.S.R.	23.0%
Canada	22.6%
New Caledonia	11.4%
Australia	7.9%
Indonesia	7.6%

▲ **Lead**

World total (1991)
5,540,000 tonnes

U.S.A.	21.6%
Former U.S.S.R.	12.1%
Germany	6.6%
Japan	6.0%
U.K.	5.6%

◖ **Chrome**

World total(1991)
13,199,000 tonnes

South Africa	34.1%
Former U.S.S.R.	28.8%
Albania	7.6%
India	7.5%
Turkey	6.4%

● **Bauxite**

World total (1991)
110,803,000 tonnes

Australia	36.6%
Guinea	15.4%
Jamaica	10.5%
Brazil	9.4%
India	4.4%

▲ **Manganese**

World total (1991)
22,000 tonnes

Former U.S.S.R.	36.4%
South Africa	14.5%
China	12.3%
Brazil	9.1%
Gabon	8.2%

▽ **Tin**

World total (1991)
195,000 tonnes

Malaysia	21.9%
Indonesia	15.6%
Brazil	15.1%
China	13.6%
Bolivia	7.5%

□ **Cobalt**

World total (1992)
28,000 tonnes

Zaïre	23.2%
Canada	16.1%
Zambia	16.1%
New Caledonia	8.9%
Australia	7.9%

◆ **Zinc**

World total (1991)
7,513,000 tonnes

Canada	15.3%
Australia	13.9%
Former U.S.S.R.	10.6%
China	9.5%
Peru	8.4%

▲ **Molybdenum**

World total (1990)
110,000 tonnes

U.S.A.	55.5%
Canada	12.3%
Chile	12.3%
Former U.S.S.R.	10.0%
Mexico	2.7%

◡ **Mercury**

World total (1991)
3,652 tonnes

Former U.S.S.R.	32.9%
China	27.4%
Mexico	19.7%
Algeria	11.8%
Slovakia	2.1%

▽ **Tungsten**

World total (1992)
30,000 tonnes

China	53.3%
Former U.S.S.R.	13.3%
North Korea	10.0%
Austria	5.2%
Mongolia	5.0%

*Some countries are highl
dependent upon minerals
The following are depend
on metals and minerals f
over 50% of the value of
their exports:*
Zambia 93%
New Caledonia 81%
Zaïre 55%

FISHING AND LAND USE

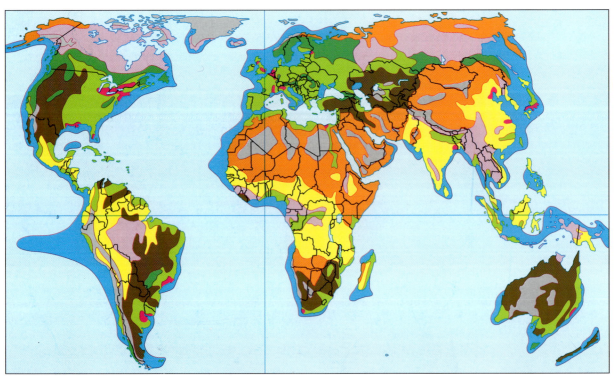

 Principal fishing areas

 Nomadic herding

 Forestry

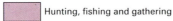 Hunting, fishing and gathering

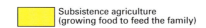 Subsistence agriculture
(growing food to feed the family)

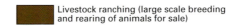 Livestock ranching (large scale breeding
and rearing of animals for sale)

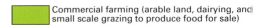 Commercial farming (arable land, dairying, and
small scale grazing to produce food for sale)

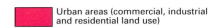 Urban areas (commercial, industrial
and residential land use)

 Unproductive land

ENERGY PRODUCTION

Primary energy production expressed in kilograms of coal equivalent per person 1992

- Over 10 000 kg per person
- 1 000 - 10 000 kg per person
- 100 - 1 000 kg per person
- 10 - 100 kg per person
- Under 10 kg per person

- ● Oil
- ▼ Natural gas
- ▲ Coal and lignite
- ◆ Uranium (the fuel used to generate nuclear power)

In most developing countries, firewood is the main source of fuel. Charcoal and dried dung are also burnt. These are called biomass fuels. The importance of these traditional fuels is shown in the pie diagrams at the foot of the page. Look at the pie diagram for Nigeria.

Projection: *Modified Hammer Equal Area*

Labels on map: Prudhoe Bay, Colorado, Texas, Appalachians, Gulf of Mexico, North Sea, Ruhr, Silesia, Donbas, Yamburg, Western Siberia, Kuzbas, Shanxi, Bihar, The Gulf, Brunei, Rum Jungle, Bowen Basin

Top 5 producers for each primary energy source with percentage of World production 1992

Oil		Natural Gas		Coal (bituminous)		Coal (lignite)		Uranium		Nuclear Power		Hydro Electric Power	
World total (1992) 3 170 000 tons		World total (1992) 2 614 000 000 tons		World total (1992) 3 120 000 000 tons		World total (1992) 1 310 000 000 tons		World total (1992) 60 000 tons		World total (1992) 461 000 000 tonnes of oil equivalent		World total (1992) 540 600 000 tonnes of oil equivalent	
former U.S.S.R.	14.2%	former U.S.S.R.	33.3%	China	35.0%	U.S.A.	22.5%	Canada	15.4%	U.S.A.	29.5%	Canada	13.8%
Saudi-Arabia	13.5%	U.S.A.	25.2%	U.S.A.	19.5%	Germany	10.5%	former U.S.S.R.	13.7%	France	15.9%	U.S.A.	12.9%
U.S.A.	13.2%	Canada	9.2%	former U.S.S.R.	15.0%	former U.S.S.R.	10.8%	Australia	6.2%	Japan	10.3%	former U.S.S.R.	10.5%
Iran	5.4%	Holland	3.0%	India	6.8%	China	6.9%	Niger	5.0%	former U.S.S.R.	10.2%	Brazil	9.7%
Mexico	4.9%	U.K.	2.6%	Australia	5.8%	Czechoslovakia	5.3%	France	3.5%	Germany	7.8%	China	5.6%

ENERGY CONSUMPTION

Primary energy consumption expressed in kilograms of coal equivalent per person 1992

- Over 10 000 kg per person
- 5 000 - 10 000 kg per person
- 1 000 - 5 000 kg per person
- 100 - 1 000 kg per person
- Under 100 kg per person

Energy consumption by Continent 1991

		Change 1990-91
Europe*	38.3%	(-0.2%)
North America	30.0%	(+2.4%)
Asia	25.0%	(+1.9%)
South America	3.0%	(-2.9%)
Africa	2.4%	(-0.4%)
Australasia	1.3%	(no change)
*includes former U.S.S.R.		

TYPE OF ENERGY CONSUMED BY SELECTED COUNTRIES 1993

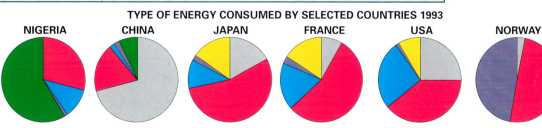

NIGERIA   CHINA   JAPAN   FRANCE   USA   NORWAY

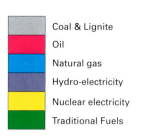

- Coal & Lignite
- Oil
- Natural gas
- Hydro-electricity
- Nuclear electricity
- Traditional Fuels

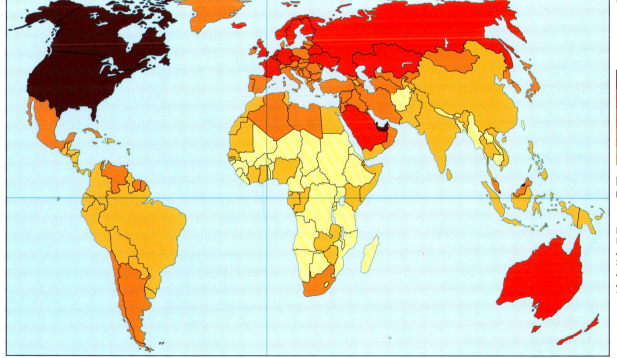

THE SEASONS

The Earth revolves around the Sun once a year in an anti-clockwise direction. It is tilted at an angle of 66½°. In June, the northern hemisphere is tilted towards the Sun. As a result it receives more hours of sunshine in a day and therefore has its warmest season, summer. By December, the Earth has rotated halfway round the Sun so that the southern hemisphere is tilted towards the Sun and it has its summer. The hemisphere that is tilted away from the Sun has winter. On 21 June the Sun is directly overhead at the Tropic of Cancer, 23½°N, and this is midsummer in the northern hemisphere. Midsummer in the southern hemisphere occurs on 21 December, when the Sun is overhead at the Tropic of Capricorn.

DAY AND NIGHT

To someone on Earth the Sun appears to rise in the east, reach its highest point at noon, and then set in the west, to be followed by night. In reality it is not the Sun that is moving but the Earth revolving from west to east. Due to the tilting of the Earth the length of day and night varies from place to place and month to month. In June the Arctic has constant daylight and the Antarctic has constant darkness. Places north of the Equator have their longest hours of daylight, and those south of the Equator their longest hours of darkness. The situations are reversed in December. In the Tropics the length of day and night varies little throughout the year.

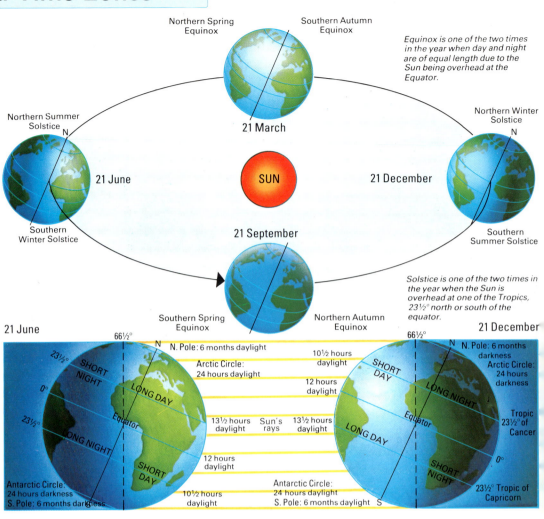

Equinox is one of the two times in the year when day and night are of equal length due to the Sun being overhead at the Equator.

Solstice is one of the two times in the year when the Sun is overhead at one of the Tropics, 23½° north or south of the equator.

TIME ZONES

The earth rotates through 360° in 24 hours, and therefore it moves 15° every hour. The world has been divided into 24 Time Zones, each centered on lines of longitude at 15° intervals, so that every country falls within one or more agreed Time Zones. The Greenwich meridian lies at the centre of the fir zone. All places to the west of this are one hour behind for every 15° longitude. All places to the east are ahead of Greenwich.

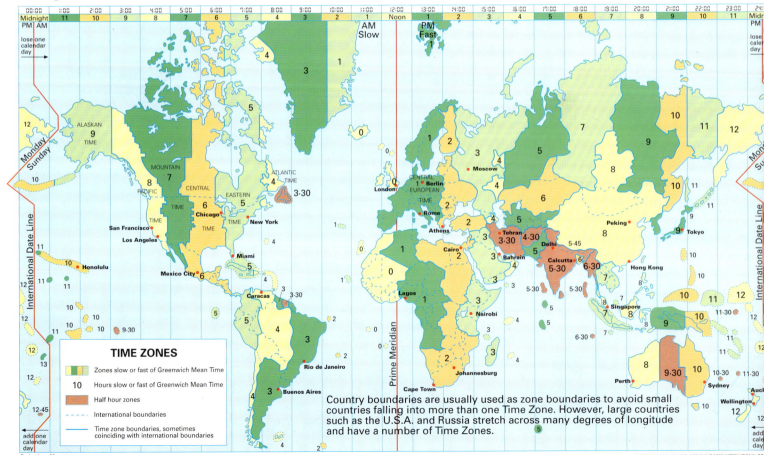

TIME ZONES

	Zones slow or fast of Greenwich Mean Time
10	Hours slow or fast of Greenwich Mean Time
	Half hour zones
------	International boundaries
——	Time zone boundaries, sometimes coinciding with international boundaries

Country boundaries are usually used as zone boundaries to avoid small countries falling into more than one Time Zone. However, large countries such as the U.S.A. and Russia stretch across many degrees of longitude and have a number of Time Zones.

This index is a list of all the names on the British Isles maps in the atlas. They are listed in alphabetical order. If a name has a description with it, for example, Point of Ayre, the name is in alphabetical order, followed by the description:

Ayre, Point of . . . .

Sometimes, the same name occurs in more than one county. In these cases, the county names are added after each place name, and they are indexed alphabetically by county.
For example:

Holy Island, Anglesey . . . .
Holy Island, Northumberland . . . . .

All rivers are indexed to their mouths or confluences and are followed by the symbol ➤.

Each name in the index is followed by a number in **bold** type which refers to the number of the page the map appears on.

The figure and letter which follow the page number give the grid rectangle on the map within which the feature appears. The grid is formed by the lines of latitude and longitude. The columns are labelled at the top and bottom with a letter and the rows at the sides with a number. Stornoway for example is in the grid square where row 1 crosses column B.

For more precise location on small scale maps the latitude and longitude are given after the figure/letter reference. The first set of figures represent the latitude, the second set of figures represent the longitude. The unit of measurement for latitude and longitude is the degree (°), which is subdivided into minutes ('). Here only full degree figures are given. The Latitude is followed by N(orth) or S(outh) of the Equator and the longitude by East or West of the prime meridian.
For example:

Stornoway . . . . . **12** 1 B 58°N 6°W

Aberdare	11	5 C	51°N	3°W
Aberdeen	12	2 F	57°N	2°W
Aberystwyth	11	4 B	52°N	4°W
Accrington	10	3 D	53°N	2°W
Achill Island	13	3 A	53°N	10°W
Airdrie	12	4 E	55°N	3°W
Aire ➤	14	5 F	53°N	0°W
Aldeburgh	11	4 H	52°N	1° E
Alderney	11	7 D	49°N	2°W
Allen, Bog of	13	3 D	53°N	7°W
Allen, Lough	13	2 C	54°N	8°W
Alnwick	10	1 E	55°N	1°W
Amlwch	10	3 B	53°N	4°W
An Uaimh	13	3 E	53°N	6°W
Anglesey	10	3 B	53°N	4°W
Annan ➤	12	4 E	54°N	3°W
Antrim	13	2 E	54°N	6°W
Antrim, Mountains of	13	2 E	54°N	6°W
Appleby	10	2 D	54°N	2°W
Aran Island	13	2 C	55°N	8°W
Aran Islands	13	3 B	53°N	9°W
Arbroath	12	3 F	56°N	2°W
Ardnamurchan, Pt. of	12	3 D	56°N	6°W
Ards Peninsula	13	2 F	54°N	5°W
Arkaig, Loch	12	3 C	56°N	5°W
Arklow	13	4 E	52°N	6°W
Armagh	13	2 E	54°N	6°W
Arran	12	4 C	55°N	5°W
Ashford	11	5 G	51°N	0° E
Ashton under Lyne	10	3 D	53°N	2°W
Athlone	13	3 D	53°N	7°W
Athy	13	4 E	53°N	7°W
Avon ➤, Bristol	11	5 D	51°N	2°W
Avon ➤, Hampshire	11	6 E	50°N	1°W
Avon ➤, Warwickshire	14	5 F	51°N	2°W
Awe, Loch	12	3 C	56°N	5°W
Aylesbury	11	5 F	51°N	0°W
Ayr	12	4 D	55°N	4°W
Ballachulish	12	3 C	56°N	5°W
Ballina	13	2 B	54°N	9°W
Ballinasloe	13	3 C	53°N	8°W
Ballycastle	13	1 E	55°N	6°W

Ballymena	13	2 E	54°N	6°W
Ballymoney	13	1 E	55°N	6°W
Balmoral	12	2 E	57°N	3°W
Banbridge	13	2 E	54°N	6°W
Banbury	11	4 E	52°N	1°W
Bandon	13	5 C	51°N	8°W
Banff	12	2 F	57°N	2°W
Bangor, Caernarfon	10	3 B	53°N	4°W
Bangor, Down	13	2 F	54°N	5°W
Bann ➤	13	2 E	54°N	6°W
Bantry	13	5 B	51°N	9°W
Bantry Bay	13	5 B	51°N	9°W
Bardsey Island	10	4 B	52°N	4°W
Barnsley	10	3 E	53°N	1°W
Barnstaple	11	5 B	51°N	4°W
Barra	12	3 A	57°N	7°W
Barrow-in-Furness	10	2 C	54°N	3°W
Barrow ➤	13	4 E	52°N	6°W
Barry	11	5 C	51°N	3°W
Basildon	11	5 G	51°N	0° E
Basingstoke	11	5 E	51°N	1°W
Bath	11	5 D	51°N	2°W
Beachy Head	11	6 G	50°N	0° E
Beauly ➤	12	2 D	57°N	4°W
Bebington	10	3 D	53°N	3°W
Bedford	11	4 F	52°N	0°W
Bedfordshire	15	5 F	52°N	0°W
Belfast	13	2 F	54°N	5°W
Belfast Lough	13	2 F	54°N	5°W
Ben Lawers	12	3 D	56°N	4°W
Ben Macdhui	12	2 E	57°N	3°W
Ben Nevis	12	3 D	56°N	4°W
Benbecula	12	2 A	57°N	7°W
Berkshire	15	6 F	51°N	1°W
Berwick-upon-Tweed	10	1 D	55°N	2°W
Bexhill	11	6 G	50°N	0° E
Billingham	10	2 E	54°N	1°W
Birkenhead	10	3 C	53°N	3°W
Birmingham	11	4 E	52°N	1°W
Bishop Auckland	10	2 E	54°N	1°W
Bishop's Stortford	11	5 G	51°N	0° E
Blackburn	10	3 D	53°N	2°W
Blackpool	10	3 C	53°N	3°W
Blackwater ➤	13	4 C	51°N	7°W

Blaenau Ffestiniog	10	4 C	52°N	3°W
Blairgowrie	12	3 E	56°N	3°W
Blarney	13	5 C	51°N	8°W
Bloody Foreland	13	1 C	55°N	8°W
Blyth	10	1 E	55°N	1°W
Bodmin Moor	11	6 B	50°N	4°W
Bog of Allen	13	3 D	53°N	7°W
Boggeragh Mountains	13	4 C	52°N	8°W
Bognor Regis	11	6 F	50°N	0°W
Bolton	10	3 D	53°N	2°W
Bootle	10	3 D	53°N	3°W
Borders	15	4 E	55°N	2°W
Boston	10	4 F	52°N	0°W
Bournemouth	11	6 E	50°N	1°W
Boyne ➤	13	3 E	53°N	6°W
Bradford	10	3 E	53°N	1°W
Brandon Mountain	13	4 A	52°N	10°W
Bray	13	3 E	53°N	6°W
Brecon	11	5 C	51°N	3°W
Brecon Beacons	11	5 C	51°N	3°W
Brentwood	11	5 G	51°N	0° E
Bressay	12	8 J	60°N	1°W
Bridlington	10	2 F	54°N	0°W
Brigg	10	3 F	53°N	0°W
Brighton	11	6 F	50°N	0°W
Bristol	11	5 D	51°N	2°W
Bristol Channel	11	5 B	51°N	4°W
Broad Law	12	4 E	55°N	3°W
Brown Willy	11	6 B	50°N	4°W
Buckie	12	2 F	57°N	2°W
Buckinghamshire	15	6 F	51°N	0°W
Buncrana	13	1 D	55°N	7°W
Bundoran	13	2 C	54°N	8°W
Bure ➤	10	4 H	52°N	1° E
Burnley	10	3 D	53°N	2°W
Burton upon Trent	10	4 E	52°N	1°W
Bury	10	3 D	53°N	2°W
Bury Saint Edmunds	11	4 G	52°N	0° E
Buxton	10	3 E	53°N	1°W
Cader Idris	10	4 C	52°N	3°W
Caernarfon	10	3 B	53°N	4°W
Caha Mountains	13	5 B	51°N	9°W

Caher	13	4 D	52°N	7°W
Cahersiveen	13	5 A	51°N	10°W
Cairn Gorm	12	2 E	57°N	3°W
Calder ➤	10	3 E	53°N	1°W
Caledonian Canal	12	2 D	56°N	5°W
Cam ➤	11	4 G	52°N	0° E
Cambrian Mountains	11	4 C	52°N	3°W
Cambridge	11	4 G	52°N	0° E
Cambridgeshire	15	5 F	52°N	0° E
Campbeltown	12	4 C	55°N	5°W
Cannock	10	4 D	52°N	2°W
Canterbury	11	5 H	51°N	1° E
Cardiff	11	5 C	51°N	3°W
Cardigan	11	4 B	52°N	4°W
Cardigan Bay	11	4 B	52°N	4°W
Carlisle	10	2 D	54°N	2°W
Carlow	13	4 E	52°N	6°W
Carmarthen	11	5 B	51°N	4°W
Carmarthen Bay	11	5 B	51°N	4°W
Garn Eige	12	2 C	57°N	5°W
Carrauntoohill	13	4 B	52°N	9°W
Carrick-on-Shannon	13	3 C	53°N	8°W
Carrick-on-Suir	13	4 D	52°N	7°W
Carrickfergus	13	2 F	54°N	5°W
Carrickmacross	13	3 E	53°N	6°W
Carron, Loch	12	2 C	57°N	5°W
Cashel	13	4 D	52°N	7°W
Castle Douglas	12	5 E	54°N	3°W
Castlebar	13	3 B	53°N	9°W
Castleford	10	3 E	53°N	1°W
Castletown Bearhaven	13	5 B	51°N	9°W
Cavan	13	3 D	54°N	7°W
Celtic Sea	14	6 B	50°N	8°W
Channel Islands	11	7 D	49°N	2°W
Chatham	11	5 G	51°N	0° E
Chelmsford	11	5 G	51°N	0° E
Cheltenham	11	5 D	51°N	2°W
Cherwell ➤	11	5 E	51°N	1°W
Cheshire	15	5 E	53°N	2°W
Chester	10	3 D	53°N	2°W
Chesterfield	10	3 E	53°N	1°W
Cheviot, The	10	1 D	55°N	2°W
Cheviot Hills	10	1 D	55°N	2°W
Chichester	11	6 F	50°N	0°W
Chiltern Hills	11	5 F	51°N	0°W

For places not in the British Isles, see World Index on pages 44 - 48

Place	Page	Grid	Lat.	Long.
Mallaig	12	**2 C**	57°N	5°W
Mallow	13	**4 C**	52°N	8°W
Malton	10	**2 F**	54°N	0°W
Man, Isle of	10	**2 B**	54°N	4°W
Manchester	10	**3 D**	53°N	2°W
Mansfield	10	**3 E**	53°N	1°W
Maree, Loch	12	**2 C**	57°N	5°W
Margate	11	**5 H**	51°N	1° E
Mask, Lough	13	**3 B**	53°N	9°W
Matlock	10	**3 E**	53°N	1°W
Mayo	15	**5 B**	53°N	9°W
Meath	15	**5 C**	53°N	6°W
Medway →	11	**5 G**	51°N	0° E
Melton Mowbray	10	**4 F**	52°N	0°W
Mendip Hills	11	**5 D**	51°N	2°W
Merrick	12	**4 D**	55°N	4°W
Mersey →	14	**5 E**	53°N	2°W
Merseyside	15	**5 E**	53°N	2°W
Merthyr Tydfil	11	**5 C**	51°N	3°W
Mid Glamorgan	15	**6 E**	51°N	3°W
Middlesbrough	10	**2 E**	54°N	1°W
Milford Haven	11	**5 A**	51°N	5°W
Milltown Malbay	13	**4 B**	52°N	9°W
Milton Keynes	11	**4 F**	52°N	0°W
Minehead	11	**5 C**	51°N	3°W
Mold	10	**3 C**	53°N	3°W
Monaghan	13	**2 E**	54°N	6°W
Monmouth	11	**5 D**	51°N	2°W
Montrose	12	**3 F**	56°N	2°W
Morar, Loch	12	**3 C**	56°N	5°W
Moray Firth	12	**2 E**	57°N	3°W
Morecambe	10	**2 D**	54°N	2°W
Morecambe Bay	10	**2 C**	54°N	3°W
Morpeth	10	**1 E**	55°N	1°W
Motherwell	12	**4 E**	55°N	4°W
Mourne Mountains	13	**2 E**	54°N	6°W
Mourne →	13	**2 D**	54°N	7°W
Moville	13	**1 D**	55°N	7°W
Mull	12	**3 C**	56°N	6°W
Mull of Galloway	12	**5 D**	54°N	4°W
Mull of Kintyre	12	**4 C**	55°N	5°W
Mullet Peninsula	13	**2 A**	54°N	10°W
Mullingar	13	**3 D**	53°N	7°W
Naas	13	**3 E**	53°N	6°W
Nairn	12	**2 E**	57°N	3°W
Neagh, Lough	13	**2 E**	54°N	6°W
Neath	11	**5 C**	51°N	3°W
Nelson	10	**3 D**	53°N	2°W
Nene →	10	**4 G**	52°N	0° E
Ness, Loch	12	**2 D**	57°N	4°W
New Forest	11	**6 E**	50°N	1°W
Newark	10	**3 F**	53°N	0°W
Newbury	11	**5 E**	51°N	1°W
Newcastle-under-Lyme	10	**3 D**	53°N	2°W
Newcastle-upon-Tyne	10	**2 E**	54°N	1°W
Newcastle West	13	**4 B**	52°N	9°W
Newhaven	11	**6 G**	50°N	0° E
Newport, Isle of Wight	11	**6 E**	50°N	1°W
Newport, Wales	11	**5 D**	51°N	3°W
Newquay	11	**6 A**	50°N	5°W
Newry	13	**2 E**	54°N	6°W
Newton Stewart	12	**5 D**	54°N	4°W
Newtown	11	**4 C**	52°N	3°W
Newtownards	13	**2 F**	54°N	5°W
Nidd →	10	**2 E**	54°N	1°W
Nith →	12	**4 E**	55°N	3°W
Nore →	13	**4 D**	52°N	7°W
Norfolk	15	**5 G**	52°N	1° E
North Downs	11	**5 G**	51°N	0° E
North Esk →	12	**3 F**	56°N	2°W
North Foreland	14	**6 G**	51°N	1° E
North Minch	12	**1 C**	58°N	5°W
North Ronaldsay	12	**7 F**	59°N	2°W
North Tyne →	10	**1 D**	54°N	2°W
North Uist	12	**2 A**	57°N	7°W
North West Highlands	12	**2 C**	57°N	5°W
North York Moors	10	**2 F**	54°N	0°W
North Yorkshire	15	**4 F**	54°N	1°W
Northallerton	10	**2 E**	54°N	1°W
Northampton	11	**4 F**	52°N	0°W
Northamptonshire	15	**5 F**	52°N	0°W
Northern Ireland	15	**4 C**	54°N	7°W
Northumberland	15	**4 E**	55°N	2°W
Norwich	10	**4 H**	52°N	1° E
Noss Head	12	**1 E**	58°N	3°W
Nottingham	10	**4 E**	52°N	1°W
Nottinghamshire	15	**5 F**	53°N	1°W
Nuneaton	11	**4 E**	52°N	1°W
Oban	12	**3 C**	56°N	5°W
Offaly	15	**5 C**	53°N	7°W
Oldham	10	**3 D**	53°N	2°W
Omagh	13	**2 D**	54°N	7°W
Orkney Isles	12	**7 E**	59°N	3°W
Oswestry	10	**4 C**	52°N	3°W
Ouse →, Cambridgeshire	11	**4 F**	52°N	0° E
Ouse →, Sussex	11	**5 G**	50°N	0° E
Ouse →, Yorkshire	10	**3 E**	53°N	0°W
Outer Hebrides	12	**2 A**	57°N	7°W
Oxford	11	**5 E**	51°N	1°W
Oxfordshire	15	**6 F**	51°N	1°W
Paisley	12	**4 D**	55°N	4°W
Peak, The	14	**5 F**	53°N	1°W
Peebles	12	**4 E**	55°N	3°W
Pembroke	11	**5 B**	51°N	4°W
Pennines	10	**2 D**	54°N	2°W
Penrith	10	**2 D**	54°N	2°W
Pentland Firth	12	**1 E**	58°N	3°W
Penzance	11	**6 A**	50°N	5°W
Perth	12	**3 E**	56°N	3°W
Peterborough	11	**4 F**	52°N	0°W
Peterhead	12	**2 G**	57°N	1°W
Pitlochry	12	**3 E**	56°N	3°W
Plymouth	11	**6 B**	50°N	4°W
Plynlimon	11	**4 C**	52°N	3°W
Pontypool	11	**5 C**	51°N	3°W
Pontypridd	11	**5 C**	51°N	3°W
Poole	11	**6 D**	50°N	1°W
Port Laoise	13	**3 D**	53°N	7°W
Port Talbot	11	**5 C**	51°N	3°W
Portadown	13	**2 E**	54°N	6°W
Portland Bill	11	**6 D**	50°N	2°W
Portree	12	**2 B**	57°N	6°W
Portsmouth	11	**6 E**	50°N	1°W
Poulaphouca Reservoir	13	**3 E**	53°N	6°W
Preston	10	**3 D**	53°N	2°W
Pwllheli	10	**4 B**	52°N	4°W
Rannoch, Loch	12	**3 D**	56°N	4°W
Rathlin Island	13	**1 E**	55°N	6°W
Reading	11	**5 F**	51°N	0°W
Redcar	10	**2 E**	54°N	1°W
Redditch	11	**4 E**	52°N	1°W
Ree, Lough	13	**3 D**	53°N	8°W
Reigate	11	**5 F**	51°N	0°W
Rhondda	11	**5 C**	51°N	3°W
Rhum	12	**3 B**	57°N	6°W
Rhyl	10	**3 C**	53°N	3°W
Ribble →	10	**3 D**	54°N	2°W
Richmond	10	**2 E**	54°N	1°W
Ripon	10	**2 E**	54°N	1°W
Rochdale	10	**3 D**	53°N	2°W
Romford	11	**5 G**	51°N	0° E
Romney Marsh	11	**5 G**	51°N	0° E
Roscommon	13	**3 C**	53°N	8°W
Roscrea	13	**4 D**	52°N	7°W
Ross-on-Wye	11	**5 D**	51°N	2°W
Rosslare	13	**4 E**	52°N	6°W
Rother →	11	**5 G**	50°N	0° E
Rotherham	10	**3 E**	53°N	1°W
Rothesay	12	**4 C**	55°N	5°W
Rousay	12	**7 E**	59°N	3°W
Rugby	11	**4 E**	52°N	1°W
Runcorn	10	**3 D**	53°N	2°W
Ryan, Loch	12	**5 C**	55°N	5°W
Rye →	10	**2 F**	54°N	0°W
Saint Albans	11	**5 F**	51°N	0°W
Saint Andrews	12	**3 F**	56°N	2°W
Saint David's Head	11	**5 A**	51°N	5°W
Saint George's Channel	13	**5 E**	52°N	6°W
Saint Helens	10	**3 D**	53°N	2°W
Saint Helier	11	**7 D**	49°N	2°W
Saint Ives	11	**6 A**	50°N	5°W
Saint Kilda	14	**3 B**	57°N	8°W
Saint Mary's	11	**8 J**	49°N	6°W
Saint Peter Port	11	**7 D**	49°N	2°W
Sale	10	**3 D**	53°N	2°W
Salford	10	**3 D**	53°N	2°W
Salisbury	11	**5 E**	51°N	1°W
Salisbury Plain	11	**5 E**	51°N	1°W
Sanday	12	**7 F**	59°N	2°W
Sark	11	**7 D**	49°N	2°W
Scafell Pike	10	**2 C**	54°N	3°W
Scarborough	10	**2 F**	54°N	0°W
Scilly Isles	11	**8 J**	49°N	6°W
Scotland	12	**3 D**	57°N	4°W
Scunthorpe	10	**3 F**	53°N	0°W
Severn →	11	**5 D**	51°N	2°W
Shannon →	13	**3 C**	52°N	9°W
Shapinsay	12	**7 F**	59°N	2°W
Sheerness	11	**5 G**	51°N	0° E
Sheffield	10	**3 E**	53°N	1°W
Shetland Isles	12	**8 J**	60°N	1°W
Shrewsbury	10	**4 D**	52°N	2°W
Shropshire	15	**5 E**	52°N	2°W
Sidmouth	11	**6 C**	50°N	3°W
Skegness	10	**3 G**	53°N	0° E
Skipton	10	**3 D**	53°N	2°W
Skye	12	**2 B**	57°N	6°W
Slaney →	13	**4 E**	52°N	6°W
Slieve Donard	13	**2 E**	54°N	5°W
Sligo	13	**2 C**	54°N	8°W
Sligo Bay	13	**2 C**	54°N	8°W
Slough	11	**5 F**	51°N	0°W
Snaefell	10	**2 B**	54°N	4°W
Snowdon	10	**3 B**	53°N	4°W
Solihull	11	**4 E**	52°N	1°W
Solway Firth	10	**2 C**	54°N	3°W
Somerset	15	**6 E**	51°N	3°W
South Downs	11	**6 F**	50°N	0°W
South Esk →	12	**3 F**	56°N	3°W
South Ronaldsay	12	**6 F**	58°N	2°W
South Shields	10	**2 E**	54°N	1°W
South Uist	12	**2 A**	57°N	7°W
South Yorkshire	15	**5 F**	53°N	1°W
Southampton	11	**6 E**	50°N	1°W
Southend	11	**5 G**	55°N	5°W
Southern Uplands	12	**4 E**	55°N	3°W
Southport	10	**3 D**	53°N	3°W
Spalding	10	**4 F**	52°N	0°W
Sperrin Mountains	13	**2 D**	54°N	7°W
Spey →	12	**2 E**	57°N	3°W
Spurn Head	10	**3 G**	53°N	0° E
Stafford	10	**4 D**	52°N	2°W
Staffordshire	15	**5 E**	52°N	2°W
Staines	11	**5 F**	51°N	0°W
Start Point	11	**6 C**	50°N	3°W
Stevenage	11	**5 F**	51°N	0°W
Stirling	12	**3 E**	56°N	3°W
Stockport	10	**3 D**	53°N	2°W
Stockton	10	**2 E**	54°N	1°W
Stoke on Trent	10	**3 D**	53°N	2°W
Stonehaven	12	**3 F**	56°N	2°W
Stonehenge	11	**5 E**	51°N	1°W
Stornoway	12	**1 B**	58°N	6°W
Stour →, Dorset	11	**6 D**	50°N	1°W
Stour →, Suffolk	11	**5 H**	51°N	1° E
Stourbridge	11	**4 D**	52°N	2°W
Strabane	13	**2 D**	54°N	7°W
Stranraer	12	**5 C**	54°N	5°W
Stratford-upon-Avon	11	**4 E**	52°N	1°W
Strath Spey	12	**2 E**	57°N	3°W
Strathmore	12	**3 E**	56°N	3°W
Stromeferry	12	**2 C**	57°N	5°W
Stronsay	12	**7 F**	59°N	2°W
Stroud	11	**5 D**	51°N	2°W
Suffolk	15	**5 G**	52°N	1° E
Suir →	14	**5 C**	52°N	7°W
Sumburgh Head	12	**7 J**	59°N	1°W
Sunderland	10	**2 E**	54°N	1°W
Surrey	15	**6 F**	51°N	0°W
Sutton Coldfield	11	**4 E**	52°N	1°W
Sutton in Ashfield	10	**3 E**	53°N	1°W
Swale →	10	**2 E**	54°N	1°W
Swanage	11	**6 D**	50°N	1°W
Swansea	11	**5 C**	51°N	3°W
Swilly, Lough	13	**1 D**	55°N	7°W
Swindon	11	**5 E**	51°N	1°W
Tamar →	11	**6 B**	50°N	4°W
Taunton	11	**5 C**	51°N	3°W
Taw →	11	**6 C**	51°N	4°W
Tay, Firth of	12	**3 F**	56°N	3°W
Tay →	12	**3 E**	56°N	3°W
Tees →	10	**2 E**	54°N	1°W
Teifi →	11	**4 B**	52°N	4°W
Teign →	11	**6 C**	50°N	3°W
Telford	10	**4 D**	52°N	2°W
Test →	11	**5 E**	51°N	1°W
Teviot →	12	**4 F**	55°N	2°W
Thame →	11	**5 E**	51°N	1°W
Thames →	11	**5 G**	51°N	0° E
Thetford	11	**4 G**	52°N	0° E
Thurso	12	**1 E**	58°N	3°W
Tipperary	13	**4 C**	52°N	8°W
Tiree	12	**3 B**	56°N	6°W
Tiverton	11	**6 C**	50°N	3°W
Tobermory	12	**3 B**	56°N	6°W
Torbay	11	**6 C**	50°N	3°W
Torquay	11	**6 C**	50°N	3°W
Torridge →	11	**6 B**	50°N	4°W
Torridon, Loch	12	**2 C**	57°N	5°W
Tralee	13	**4 B**	52°N	9°W
Tramore	13	**4 D**	52°N	7°W
Trawsfynydd, Lake	14	**5 D**	52°N	3°W
Trent →	10	**3 F**	53°N	0°W
Trowbridge	11	**5 D**	51°N	2°W
Truro	11	**6 A**	50°N	5°W
Tullamore	13	**3 D**	53°N	7°W
Tunbridge Wells	11	**5 G**	51°N	0° E
Turriff	12	**2 F**	57°N	2°W
Tweed →	12	**4 F**	55°N	1°W
Tyne and Wear	15	**4 F**	54°N	1°W
Tyne →	10	**2 E**	54°N	1°W
Tynemouth	10	**1 E**	55°N	1°W
Tyrone (county)	15	**4 C**	54°N	7°W
Tywi →	11	**5 B**	51°N	4°W
Ullapool	12	**2 C**	57°N	5°W
Unst	12	**8 K**	60°N	0°W
Upper Lough Erne	13	**2 D**	54°N	7°W
Ure →	10	**2 E**	54°N	1°W
Usk →	11	**5 C**	51°N	2°W
Valencia Island	13	**5 A**	51°N	10°W
Vyrnwy, Lake	10	**4 C**	52°N	3°W
Wakefield	10	**3 E**	53°N	1°W
Wales	11	**4 C**	52°N	3°W
Wallasey	10	**3 C**	53°N	3°W
Walney, Isle of	10	**2 C**	54°N	3°W
Walsall	11	**4 E**	52°N	1°W
Warrenpoint	13	**2 E**	54°N	6°W
Warrington	10	**3 D**	53°N	2°W
Warwick	11	**4 E**	52°N	1°W
Warwickshire	15	**5 F**	52°N	1°W
Wash, The	10	**3 G**	52°N	0° E
Washington	10	**2 E**	54°N	1°W
Waterford	13	**4 D**	52°N	7°W
Watford	11	**5 F**	51°N	0°W
Waveney →	11	**4 H**	52°N	1° E
Wear →	10	**2 D**	54°N	1°W
Welland →	11	**4 F**	52°N	0°W
Wellingborough	11	**4 F**	52°N	0°W
Wells	10	**4 G**	52°N	0° E
Welshpool	11	**4 C**	52°N	3°W
Welwyn Garden City	11	**5 F**	51°N	0°W
Wensleydale	10	**2 E**	54°N	2°W
West Bromwich	11	**4 D**	52°N	2°W
West Midlands	15	**5 E**	52°N	1°W
West Sussex	15	**6 F**	50°N	0°W
West Yorkshire	15	**5 F**	53°N	1°W
Western Isles	15	**3 C**	57°N	7°W
Westmeath	15	**5 C**	53°N	7°W
Weston-super-Mare	11	**5 D**	51°N	2°W
Westport	13	**3 B**	53°N	9°W
Westray	12	**7 F**	59°N	3°W
Wexford	13	**4 E**	52°N	6°W
Weymouth	11	**6 D**	50°N	2°W
Whalsay	12	**8 K**	60°N	1°W
Wharfe →	10	**3 E**	53°N	1°W
Wharfedale	10	**2 D**	54°N	2°W
Whernside	10	**2 D**	54°N	2°W
Whitby	10	**2 F**	54°N	0°W
Whitehaven	10	**2 C**	54°N	3°W
Wick	12	**1 E**	58°N	3°W
Wicklow	13	**4 E**	53°N	6°W
Wicklow Mountains	13	**4 E**	53°N	6°W
Widnes	10	**3 D**	53°N	2°W
Wigan	10	**3 D**	53°N	2°W
Wight, Isle of	11	**6 E**	50°N	1°W
Wigtown	12	**5 D**	54°N	4°W
Wiltshire	15	**6 F**	51°N	2°W
Winchester	11	**5 E**	51°N	1°W
Windermere	10	**2 D**	54°N	2°W
Windrush →	11	**5 E**	51°N	1°W
Windsor	11	**5 F**	51°N	0°W
Witham →	10	**3 F**	53°N	0°W
Withernsea	10	**3 G**	53°N	0° E
Woking	11	**5 F**	51°N	0°W
Wolverhampton	11	**4 D**	52°N	2°W
Worcester	11	**4 D**	52°N	2°W
Workington	10	**2 C**	54°N	3°W
Worksop	10	**3 E**	53°N	1°W
Worthing	11	**6 F**	50°N	0°W
Wrath, Cape	12	**1 C**	58°N	5°W
Wrexham	10	**3 C**	53°N	3°W
Wye →	11	**5 D**	51°N	2°W
Yare →	11	**4 H**	52°N	1° E
Yell	12	**8 J**	60°N	1°W
Yeo →	11	**5 D**	51°N	3°W
Yeovil	11	**6 D**	50°N	2°W
York	10	**3 E**	53°N	1°W
Yorkshire Wolds	10	**2 F**	54°N	0°W
Youghal	13	**5 D**	51°N	7°W

For places not in the British Isles, see World Index on pages 44 - 48

CARTOGRAPHY BY PHILIP'S. COPYRIGHT REED INTERNATIONAL BOOKS LTD

This index is a list of the names on the regional maps in the World Map Section of the atlas. They are listed in alphabetical order. If a name has a description with it, for example, Bay of Biscay, the name is in alphabetical order, followed by the description:

Biscay, Bay of . . . .

Sometimes, the same name occurs in more than one country. In these cases, the country names are added after each place name, and they are indexed alphabetically by country.
For example:

Cordoba, Argentina . . .
Cordoba, Spain . . . .

All rivers are indexed to their mouths or confluences, and are followed by the symbol ➔.

Each name in the index is followed by a number in **bold** type which refers to the number of the page the map appears on.

The figure and letter which follow the page number give the grid rectangle on the map within which the feature appears. The grid is formed by the lines of latitude and longitude. The columns are labelled at the top and bottom with a letter and the rows at the sides with a number. Poznan, for example, is in the grid rectangle where row 5 crosses column D.

For more precise location on small scale maps the latitude and longitude are given after the figure/letter reference. The first set of figures represent the latitude, the second set of figures represent the longitude.

The unit of measurement for latitude and longitude is the degree (°), which is subdivided into minutes ('). Here only full degree figures are given. The latitude is followed by N(orth) or S(outh) of the Equator and the longitude by E(ast) or W(est) of the prime meridian.
For example:

Poznan . . . . . .**3 5D** 52°N 16°W

Aalborg	4	4P	57°N	9° E
Aarhus	4	4P	56°N	10° E
Abadan	12	3C	30°N	48° E
Aberdeen	4	4G	57°N	2°W
Abidjan	14	4C	5°N	3°W
Abu Dhabi	12	4D	24°N	54° E
Abuja	15	10M	9°N	7° E
Acapulco	22	4D	16°N	99°W
Accra	15	10K	5°N	0°W
Aconcagua	19	7E	32°S	70°W
Adamawa Highlands	15	10N	7°N	12° E
Adana	7	4L	37°N	35° E
Addis Ababa	14	4G	9°N	38° E
Adelaide	16	6F	34°S	138° E
Aden	12	5C	12°N	45° E
Aden, Gulf of	12	5C	12°N	47° E
Adriatic Sea	6	3F	43°N	16° E
Aegean Sea	7	4J	38°N	25° E
Afghanistan	12	3E	33°N	65° E
Africa	14	5F	10°N	20° E
Agades	14	3D	16°N	7° E
Agra	12	4F	27°N	77° E
Aguanaval ➔	22	3D	25°N	102°W
Aguascalientes	22	3D	21°N	102°W
Ahmadabad	12	4F	23°N	72° E
Aix-en-Provence	5	11L	43°N	5° E
Ajaccio	5	12N	41°N	8° E
Akita	11	3D	39°N	140° E
Al Hufuf	12	4C	25°N	49° E
Alabama	21	4J	33°N	87°W
Åland Islands	3	3D	60°N	20° E
Alaska	18	3D	65°N	150°W
Alaska, Gulf of	18	4E	58°N	145°W
Alaska Peninsula	18	4C	56°N	160°W
Alaska Range	18	3D	62°N	151°W
Albacete	5	13H	39°N	1°W
Albania	7	3G	41°N	20° E
Albany	16	6B	35°S	117° E
Albuquerque	20	3E	35°N	106°W
Aldabra Islands	14	5H	9°S	46° E
Ålesund	3	3B	62°N	6° E
Aleutian Islands	17	2K	52°N	175°W
Alexandria	14	1G	31°N	30° E
Algeria	14	2D	28°N	2° E
Algiers	14	1D	36°N	3° E
Alicante	5	13H	38°N	0°W
Alice Springs	16	4E	23°S	133° E
Allahabad	12	4G	25°N	81° E
Allegheny Mountains	21	3L	38°N	80°W
Alma Ata	8	8E	43°N	76° E
Almeria	5	14G	36°N	2°W
Alps	5	9N	46°N	9° E
Altai	8	9D	46°N	92° E
Amazon ➔	19	4E	0°S	50°W
America, North	18	5K	45°N	100°W
America, South	19	5F	10°S	60°W
Amiens	5	8J	49°N	2° E
Amritsar	12	3F	31°N	74° E
Amsterdam	4	6L	52°N	4° E
Amu Darya ➔	8	6E	43°N	59° E
Amur ➔	9	15D	52°N	141° E
Anadyr Range	9	18C	68°N	175° E
Anchorage	18	3E	61°N	149°W
Andaman Islands	13	5H	12°N	92° E
Andes	19	5D	10°S	75°W
Andizhan	8	8E	41°N	72° E
Andorra	5	11J	42°N	1° E
Angara ➔	9	10D	58°N	94° E
Angel Falls	19	3E	5°N	62°W
Angola	14	6E	12°S	18° E
Ankara	7	4K	39°N	32° E
Antananarivo	15	6H	18°S	47° E
Antarctic Peninsula	24	L	67°S	60°W
Antarctica	24	D	90°S	0° E
Antigua	23	4M	17°N	61°W
Antofagasta	19	6D	23°S	70°W
Antwerp	4	7L	51°N	4° E
Aomori	11	2D	40°N	140° E
Apennines	5	11P	44°N	10° E
Appalachian Mountains	21	3K	38°N	80°W
Arabian Sea	12	5E	16°N	65° E
Aracajú	19	5H	10°S	37°W
Arafura Sea	16	2E	9°S	135° E
Aral Sea	8	6E	44°N	60° E
Ararat, Mount	2	8Q	39°N	44° E
Arctic Ocean	24	B	78°N	160°W
Arequipa	19	5D	16°S	71°W
Argentina	19	7E	35°S	66°W
Arizona	20	4D	34°N	112°W
Arkansas	21	4H	35°N	92°W
Arkansas ➔	21	4H	33°N	91°W
Arkhangelsk	3	3J	64°N	41° E
Armenia	8	5E	40°N	45° E
Arnhem	4	7L	51°N	5° E
Arnhem Land	16	2E	13°S	134° E
Ascension	26	4J	8°S	14°W
Ashkhabad	8	6F	38°N	57° E
Asmara	14	3G	15°N	38° E
Assam	13	4H	26°N	93° E
Astrakhan	8	5D	46°N	48° E
Asunción	19	6F	25°S	57°W
Aswan	14	2G	24°N	32° E
Atacama Desert	19	6D	24°S	69°W
Athens	7	4H	37°N	23° E
Atlanta	21	4K	33°N	84°W
Atlantic Ocean	26	3H	0°	20°W
Atlas Mountains	14	1C	32°N	5°W
Auckland	16	10M	36°S	174° E
Augsburg	5	8P	48°N	10° E
Australia	16	4E	23°S	135° E
Australian Alps	16	7H	36°S	148° E
Austria	6	2F	47°N	14° E
Avignon	5	11L	43°N	4° E
Azerbaijan	8	5E	40°N	48° E
Azores	26	2H	38°N	29°W
Azov, Sea of	7	2L	46°N	36° E
Baffin Bay	18	2N	72°N	64°W
Baffin Island	18	2M	68°N	75°W
Baghdad	12	3C	33°N	44° E
Bahamas	23	3J	24°N	75°W
Bahía Blanca	19	7E	38°S	62°W
Bahrain	12	4D	26°N	50° E
Baikal, Lake	9	11D	53°N	108° E
Baku	8	6E	40°N	49° E
Balearic Islands	5	13J	39°N	3° E
Bali	13	7K	8°S	115° E
Balkan Mountains	7	3H	43°N	23° E
Balkhash, Lake	8	8E	46°N	74° E
Ballarat	16	7G	37°S	143° E
Baltic Sea	3	4D	57°N	19° E
Baltimore	21	3L	39°N	76°W
Bamako	14	3C	12°N	7°W
Banda Sea	13	7L	6°S	130° E
Bandung	13	7J	6°S	107° E
Bangka	13	7J	2°S	105° E
Bangalore	12	5F	12°N	77° E
Bangkok	13	5J	13°N	100° E
Bangladesh	13	4H	24°N	90° E
Bangui	14	3E	4°N	18° E
Banjarmasin	13	7K	3°S	114° E
Banjul	14	3B	13°N	16°W
Barbados	23	5N	13°N	59°W
Barcelona	5	12K	41°N	2° E
Barcoo ➔	16	4G	25°S	142° E
Barents Sea	8	4B	73°N	39° E
Bari	7	3G	41°N	16° E
Barkly Tableland	16	3F	17°S	136° E
Barquisimeto	23	5L	10°N	69°W
Barranquilla	23	5K	11°N	74°W
Basle	5	9M	47°N	7° E
Basra	12	3C	30°N	47° E
Bass Strait	16	7H	39°S	146° E
Batumi	7	3M	41°N	41° E
Bayonne	5	11H	43°N	1°W
Beaufort Sea	18	2E	72°N	140°W
Beijing	13	3K	39°N	116° E
Beira	15	6G	19°S	34° E
Belarus	3	5F	53°N	27° E
Belém	19	4G	1°S	48°W
Belfast	4	5F	54°N	5°W
Belgium	4	7K	50°N	5° E
Belgrade	7	3H	44°N	20° E
Belize	22	4G	17°N	88°W
Bellingshausen Sea	24	L	66°S	80°W
Belmopan	22	4G	17°N	88°W
Belo Horizonte	19	5G	19°S	43°W
Bendigo	16	7G	36°S	144° E
Bengal, Bay of	13	5H	15°N	90° E
Benghazi	14	1F	32°N	20° E
Benin	15	10L	10°N	2° E
Benin, Bight of	15	10L	5°N	3° E
Benin City	15	10M	6°N	5° E
Benue ➔	15	10M	7°N	6° E
Bergen	3	3B	60°N	5° E
Bering Sea	17	2L	58°N	171° E
Bering Strait	18	2C	66°N	170°W
Berlin	4	6Q	52°N	13° E
Bermuda	23	1M	32°N	65°W
Berne	5	9M	46°N	7° E
Bhutan	13	4H	27°N	90° E
Bialystok	3	5E	53°N	23° E
Bié Plateau	14	6E	12°S	16° E
Bielefeld	4	6N	52°N	8° E
Bilbao	5	11G	43°N	2°W
Bioko	15	11M	3°N	8° E
Birmingham	4	6H	52°N	1°W
Biscay, Bay of	5	10F	45°N	2°W
Bishkek	8	8E	42°N	74° E

For places within the British Isles, see British Isles Index on pages 41 - 43

Bismarck Archipelago .. 17 8H 2°S 150° E
Bissau .... 14 3B 11°N 15°W
Black Sea ... 7 3K 43°N 35° E
Blanc, Mont . 5 10M 45°N 6° E
Blantyre ..... 14 6G 15°S 35° E
Bloemfontein .. 15 7F 29°S 26° E
Blue Nile → .. 14 3G 15°N 32° E
Bobo-Dioulasso . 14 3C 11°N 4°W
Bodø .... 3 2C 67°N 14° E
Bogotá .... 23 7K 4°N 74°W
Bolivia .... 19 5E 17°S 64°W
Bologna .... 5 10P 44°N 11° E
Bolzano .... 5 9P 46°N 11° E
Bombay .... 12 5F 18°N 72° E
Bonn ..... 4 7M 50°N 7° E
Bordeaux .... 5 10H 44°N 0°W
Borneo .... 13 6K 1°N 115° E
Bornholm .... 3 4C 55°N 15° E
Bosnia- Herzegovina . 7 3G 44°N 17° E
Bosporus .... 7 3J 41°N 29° E
Boston .... 21 2M 42°N 71°W
Bothnia, Gulf of . 3 5E 63°N 20° E
Botswana .... 15 7F 22°S 24° E
Bourges .... 5 9K 47°N 2° E
Brahmaputra → . 13 4H 23°N 89° E
Brasília .... 19 5G 15°S 47°W
Brasov .... 7 2J 45°N 25° E
Bratislava .... 2 6K 48°N 17° E
Brazil .... 19 4F 12°S 50°W
Brazzaville .... 14 5E 4°S 15° E
Bremen ..... 4 6N 53°N 8° E
Brest, Belarus . 3 5E 52°N 23° E
Brest, France . 5 8F 48°N 4°W
Bridgetown.... 23 5N 13°N 59°W
Brisbane .... 16 5J 27°S 153° E
Bristol .... 4 7G 51°N 2°W
British Isles .. 26 2J 54°N 4°W
Brno ..... 7 2G 49°N 16° E
Broken Hill .. 16 6G 31°S 141° E
Brooks Range . 18 3D 68°N 147°W
Broome .... 16 3C 18°S 122° E
Brunei .... 13 6K 4°N 115° E
Brunswick .... 4 6P 52°N 10° E
Brussels .... 4 7L 50°N 4° E
Bryansk .... 3 5G 53°N 34° E
Bucaramanga .. 19 3D 7°N 73°W
Bucharest .... 7 3J 44°N 26° E
Budapest ..... 7 2G 47°N 19° E
Buenos Aires .. 19 7F 34°S 58°W
Buffalo .... 21 2L 42°N 78°W
Bujumbura ... 14 5F 3°S 29° E
Bulawayo .... 15 7F 20°S 28° E
Bulgaria .... 7 3H 42°N 25° E
Bundaberg .... 16 4J 24°S 152° E
Burkina Faso .. 14 3C 12°N 1°W
Burma .... 13 4H 21°N 96° E
Bursa .... 7 3J 40°N 29° E
Buru .... 13 7L 3°S 126° E
Burundi .... 14 5F 3°S 30° E
Bydgoszcz ... 3 5D 53°N 18° E

Cadiz ..... 5 14E 36°N 6°W
Caen ..... 5 8H 49°N 0°W
Cagliari .... 5 13N 39°N 9° E
Cairns .... 16 3H 16°S 145° E
Cairo .... 14 1G 30°N 31° E
Calais .... 4 7J 50°N 1° E
Calcutta .... 12 4G 22°N 88° E
Calgary .... 18 4H 51°N 114°W
Cali .... 23 7J 3°N 76°W
California .... 20 3B 37°N 119°W
California, Gulf of 22 2B 27°N 111°W
Cambodia .... 13 5J 12°N 105° E
Cameroon .... 14 4E 6°N 12° E
Cameroon, Mount 15 11M 4°N 9° E
Campeche, Gulf of .... 22 3F 19°N 93°W
Campinas ..... 19 6G 22°S 47°W
Campo Grande . 19 6F 20°S 54°W
Canada.... 18 4K 60°N 100°W
Canary Islands . 14 2B 28°N 16°W
Canberra .... 16 7H 35°S 149° E
Cantabrian Mountains .. 5 11F 43°N 5°W
Canton .... 13 4K 23°N 113° E
Cape Town .. 15 8E 33°S 18° E
Cape Verde Islands ..26 3H 17°N 25°W
Cape York Peninsula .. 16 2G 12°S 142° E
Caracas ..23 5L 10°N 66°W
Cardiff .... 4 7G 51°N 3°W
Caribbean Sea . 23 5J 15°N 75°W
Caroline Islands .17 7H 8°N 150° E
Carpathians .. 7 2H 49°N 21° E
Carpentaria, Gulf of .... 16 2F 14°S 139° E

Cartagena, Colombia .... 23 5J 10°N 75°W
Cartagena, Spain 5 14H 37°N 0°W
Casablanca ... 14 1C 33°N 7°W
Caspian Sea ... 8 6F 43°N 50° E
Catalonia .... 6 3D 41°N 1° E
Catania .... 6 4F 37°N 15° E
Caucasus .... 8 5E 42°N 44° E
Cayenne ...... 19 3F 5°N 52°W
Cebu .... 13 5L 10°N 123° E
Celebes .... 13 7L 2°S 120° E
Celebes Sea.... 13 6L 3°N 123° E
Central African Republic ..... 14 4E 7°N 20° E
Central America . 26 3C 10°N 85°W
Ceylon .... 27 3P 7°N 80° E
Chad .... 14 3E 15°N 17° E
Chad, Lake .. 14 3E 13°N 14° E
Changchun.... 13 2L 43°N 125° E
Changsha .... 13 4K 28°N 113° E
Channel Islands . 5 8G 49°N 2°W
Charlotte .... 21 3K 35°N 80°W
Chelyabinsk .... 8 7D 55°N 61° E
Chelyuskin, Cape 9 11B 77°N 103° E
Chemnitz .... 4 7Q 50°N 12° E
Chengdu .... 13 3J 30°N 104° E
Cherbourg .... 5 8H 49°N 1°W
Cherepovets.... 3 4H 59°N 37° E
Cherskiy .... 24 B 68°N 161° E
Chicago .... 21 2J 41°N 87°W
Chiengmai .... 13 5H 18°N 98° E
Chihuahua .... 22 2C 28°N 106°W
Chile .... 19 7D 35°S 72°W
China .... 13 3J 30°N 110° E
Chisinau .... 7 2J 47°N 28° E
Chita .... 9 12D 52°N 113° E
Chittagong .... 13 4H 22°N 91° E
Christchurch .. 16 11M 43°S 172° E
Chudskoye, Lake 3 4F 58°N 27° E
Chungking .... 13 4J 29°N 106° E
Cincinnati .... 21 3K 39°N 84°W
Citlaltepetl .... 22 4E 19°N 97°W
Ciudad Bolívar 23 6M 8°N 63°W
Ciudad Guayana 19 3E 8°N 62°W
Ciudad Juarez .. 22 1C 31°N 106°W
Clermont-Ferrand 5 10K 45°N 3° E
Cleveland .... 21 2K 41°N 81°W
Cluj-Napoca .. 7 2H 46°N 23° E
Coimbatore .. 12 5F 11°N 76° E
Cologne ..... 4 7M 50°N 6° E
Colombia .... 19 3D 3°N 73°W
Colombo .... 12 6F 6°N 79° E
Colorado .... 20 3E 39°N 105°W
Colorado Plateau 20 3D 36°N 110°W
Colorado Springs 20 3F 38°N 104°W
Colorado → .. 20 4D 28°N 95°W
Columbia → .. 20 1B 46°N 124°W
Columbus .... 21 3K 39°N 83°W
Comorin, Cape . 12 6F 8°N 77° E
Comoros .... 14 6H 12°S 44° E
Conakry .... 14 4B 9°N 13°W
Concepcion .. 19 7D 36°S 73°W
Congo .... 14 5E 1°S 16° E
Congo Basin .. 14 5F 0°S 24° E
Connecticut .. 21 2M 41°N 72°W
Constance, Lake 5 9N 47°N 9° E
Constanța .... 7 3J 44°N 28° E
Constantine .. 14 1D 36°N 6° E
Cook, Mount .. 16 11M 43°S 170° E
Cook Islands .. 17 10N 17°S 160°W
Cook Strait .... 16 11M 41°S 174° E
Copenhagen .. 4 5Q 55°N 12° E
Coral Sea .... 16 3J 15°S 150° E
Cordoba, Argentina .... 19 7E 31°S 64°W
Cordoba, Spain . 5 14F 37°N 4°W
Corfu .... 7 4G 39°N 19° E
Corinth, Gulf of . 7 4H 38°N 22° E
Cork .... 4 7D 51°N 8°W
Corrientes, Cape 22 3C 20°N 105°W
Corsica .... 5 11N 42°N 9° E
Costa Brava .. 6 3D 41°N 3° E
Costa del Sol ... 6 4C 36°N 4°W
Costa Rica .. 23 5H 10°N 84°W
Crete .... 7 4H 35°N 25° E
Crimea .... 7 2K 45°N 34° E
Croatia .... 7 2G 45°N 17° E
Cuba .... 23 3J 22°N 79°W
Cuenca .... 19 4D 2°S 79°W
Culiacan .... 22 3C 24°N 107°W
Curacao .... 19 2E 12°N 69°W
Curitiba .... 19 6G 25°S 49°W
Cuzco .... 19 5D 13°S 72°W
Cyprus .... 7 4K 35°N 33° E
Czech Republic . 6 2F 50°N 15° E

Da Nang .... 13 5J 16°N 108° E
Dacca .... 13 4H 23°N 90° E
Dakar .... 14 3B 14°N 17°W

Dalian .... 13 3L 38°N 121° E
Dallas .... 21 4G 32°N 96°W
Danube → ... 7 3J 45°N 29° E
Dar es Salaam .. 14 5G 6°S 39° E
Dardanelles ... 7 3J 40°N 26° E
Darién, Gulf of .. 23 6J 9°N 77°W
Darling Range .. 16 6B 32°S 116° E
Darling → ... 16 6G 34°S 141° E
Darwin ..... 16 2E 12°S 130° E
Davao ..... 13 6L 7°N 125° E
Davis Strait .. 18 3P 65°N 58°W
Death Valley .. 20 3C 36°N 116°W
Debrecen ..... 7 2H 47°N 21° F
Deccan ..... 12 5F 18°N 79° E
Delaware .. 21 3L 39°N 75°W
Delhi ..... 12 4F 28°N 77° E
Denmark .... 4 5N 55°N 9° E
Denmark Strait .. 18 3S 66°N 30°W
Denver ..... 20 3F 39°N 105°W
Detroit ..... 21 2K 42°N 83°W
Dijon ..... 5 9L 47°N 5° E
Dinaric Alps .. 7 3G 44°N 16° E
Djibouti ..... 14 3H 12°N 43° E
Dnepr → ... 7 1K 46°N 32° E
Dnepropetrovsk . 7 2K 48°N 35° E
Dnestr → ... 7 2J 46°N 30° E
Dodecanese ... 7 4J 36°N 27° E
Dodoma ..... 14 5G 6°S 35° E
Dominica ..... 23 4M 15°N 61°W
Dominican Republic ..... 23 4K 19°N 70°W
Don → .... 8 5E 47°N 39° E
Donetsk ..... 7 2L 48°N 37° E
Dortmund .... 4 7M 51°N 7° E
Douala ..... 15 11M 4°N 9° E
Douro → .... 5 12D 41°N 8°W
Drakensberg .. 15 7F 31°S 28° E
Drammen .... 3 4C 59°N 10° E
Drava → ... 7 2G 45°N 18° E
Dresden .... 4 7Q 51°N 13° E
Dublin ..... 4 6E 53°N 6°W
Dubrovnik .. 7 3G 42°N 18° E
Duero → ... 5 12F 41°N 0°W
Dundee ..... 4 4G 56°N 3°W
Dunedin .... 16 12M 45°S 170° E
Durango .... 22 3D 24°N 104°W
Durban .... 15 7G 29°S 31° E
Dushanbe .. 8 7F 38°N 68° E
Düsseldorf .. 4 7M 51°N 6° E
Dvina, North → . 8 5C 64°N 40° E
Dvina, West → . 3 4F 56°N 24° E
Dzungaria ..... 13 2G 44°N 88° E

East China Sea . 13 4L 30°N 126° E
East Indies .... 13 7K 0° 120° E
East London..... 15 8F 33°S 27° E
East Siberian Sea 9 16B 73°N 160° E
Easter Island .. 17 10T 27°S 109°W
Eastern Ghats .. 12 5F 14°N 78° E
Ebro → ... 5 12J 40°N 0° E
Ecuador ..... 19 4D 2°S 78°W
Edinburgh..... 4 5G 55°N 3°W
Edmonton .... 18 4H 53°N 113°W
Egypt ..... 14 2G 28°N 31° E
El Aaiun .. 14 2B 27°N 13°W
El Obeid ..... 14 3G 13°N 30° E
El Salvador .. 22 5G 13°N 89°W
Elba .... 5 11P 42°N 10° E
Elbe → .... 4 6P 53°N 9° E
Elbert, Mount .. 20 3E 39°N 106°W
Elbrus, Mount .. 2 7Q 43°N 42° E
Ellesmere Island . 18 2M 79°N 80°W
England ..... 4 6G 53°N 2°W
English Channel . 4 7H 50°N 2°W
Enugu ..... 15 10M 6°N 7° E
Equatorial Guinea 14 4D 2°N 8° E
Erfurt ..... 4 7P 50°N 11° E
Erie, Lake .. 21 2K 42°N 81°W
Eritrea .... 14 3G 14°N 38° E
Esbjerg .... 4 5N 55°N 8° E
Esfahan ..... 12 3D 33°N 51° E
Essen .... 4 7M 51°N 6° E
Essequibo → . 23 6N 6°N 58°W
Estonia .... 3 4F 58°N 25° E
Ethiopia .... 14 4H 8°N 40° E
Ethiopian Highlands .... 14 4G 10°N 37° E
Etna, Mount .. 6 4F 37°N 15° E
Euphrates →.. 12 3C 31°N 47° E
Everest, Mount.. 12 4G 28°N 86° E
Everglades, The . 21 5K 25°N 81°W
Eyre, Lake .. 16 5F 29°S 137° E

Faisalabad .... 12 3F 31°N 73° E
Falkland Islands . 19 9F 51°S 59°W
Farewell, Cape .. 18 4Q 59°N 43°W
Faroe Islands ... 4 2E 62°N 7°W
Fès .... 14 1C 34°N 5°W

Fiji .... 17 9K 17°S 179° E
Finland .... 3 3F 63°N 27° E
Finland, Gulf of . 3 4F 60°N 26° E
Flensburg .... 4 5N 54°N 9° E
Flinders Island . 16 7H 40°S 148° E
Flinders Ranges . 16 6F 31°S 138° E
Florence .... 5 11P 43°N 11° E
Flores Sea .... 13 7K 6°S 120° E
Florida .... 21 5K 28°N 82°W
Florida Keys .. 21 6K 24°N 81°W
Florida Strait .. 23 5L 25°N 80°W
Fort-de-France .. 23 5M 14°N 61°W
Fort Worth .. 21 4G 32°N 97°W
Fortaleza .... 19 4H 3°S 38°W
France .... 5 9J 47°N 3° E
Frankfurt ..... 4 7N 50°N 8° E
Franz Josef Land 24 F 81°N 60° E
Fredrikstad .... 3 4C 59°N 10° E
Freetown .... 14 4B 8°N 13°W
Freiburg .... 5 8M 48°N 7° E
Fremantle .... 16 6B 32°S 115° E
French Guiana . 19 3F 4°N 53°W
Frisian Islands . 4 6L 53°N 6° E
Fukuoka .... 11 4B 33°N 130° E
Fukushima .. 11 3D 37°N 140° E
Fushun .... 13 2L 41°N 123° E
Fuzhou .... 13 4K 26°N 119° E

Gabon .... 14 5E 0°S 10° E
Gaborone .... 15 7F 24°S 25° E
Gairdner, Lake . 16 6F 31°S 136° E
Galapagos Islands .... 19 4B 0°N 89°W
Galati .... 7 2J 45°N 28° E
Galdhøpiggen . 3 3B 61°N 8° E
Gambia .... 14 3B 13°N 16°W
Ganges → ... 12 4J 23°N 90° E
Garonne → .. 5 10H 45°N 0°W
Gävle .... 3 3D 60°N 17° E
Gaziantep .... 7 4L 37°N 37° E
Gdansk .... 3 5D 54°N 18° E
Geelong .... 16 7G 38°S 144° E
Geneva .... 5 9M 46°N 6° E
Geneva, Lake . 5 9M 46°N 6° E
Genoa .... 5 10N 44°N 8° E
Genoa, Gulf of . 5 11N 44°N 9° E
George Town .. 13 6J 5°N 100° E
Georgetown .. 23 6N 6°N 58°W
Georgia, Asia . 8 5E 42°N 43° E
Georgia, USA . 21 4K 32°N 83°W
Geraldton .... 16 5A 28°S 114° E
Germany .... 4 7N 52°N 10° E
Ghana .... 15 10K 8°N 1°W
Ghats, Eastern . 12 5F 14°N 78°E
Ghent .... 4 7K 51°N 3° E
Gibraltar .... 5 14F 36°N 5°W
Gibraltar, Strait of 5 14E 35°N 5°W
Gibson Desert . 16 4C 24°S 126° E
Gifu .... 11 3C 35°N 136° E
Gijon .... 5 11F 43°N 5°W
Gironde → ... 5 10H 45°N 1°W
Gladstone .. 16 4J 23°S 151° E
Glasgow .... 4 5F 55°N 4°W
Gobi .... 9 11E 44°N 111° E
Godavari → ... 12 5F 16°N 82° E
Godthab .... 18 3P 64°N 51°W
Goiânia .... 19 5G 16°S 49°W
Gold Coast .. 16 5J 28°S 153° E
Gomel .... 3 5G 52°N 31° E
Good Hope, Cape of .... 15 8E 34°S 18° E
Gotaland .... 3 4C 58°N 14° E
Gothenburg ... 3 4C 40°N 100°W
Gotland .... 3 4D 57°N 18° E
Gran Chaco .. 19 6E 25°S 61°W
Granada .... 5 14G 37°N 3°W
Grand Bahama Island .... 23 2J 26°N 78°W
Grand Canyon .. 20 3D 36°N 112°W
Grand Cayman .. 23 4H 19°N 81°W
Graz .... 7 2G 47°N 15° E
Great Australian Bight .... 16 6D 33°S 130° E
Great Barrier Reef 16 3H 18°S 146° E
Great Basin .. 20 3C 39°N 116°W
Great Bear Lake . 18 3G 65°N 120°W
Great Divide .. 16 6J 23°S 146° E
Great Khingan Mountains .. 13 2L 47°N 121° E
Great Lakes .. 18 5L 46°N 85°W
Great Plains .. 20 1E 47°N 105°W
Great Salt Lake . 20 2D 41°N 112°W
Great Salt Lake Desert ..... 20 3D 40°N 113°W
Great Sandy Desert .... 16 4C 21°S 124° E
Great Slave Lake 18 3H 61°N 115°W
Great Victoria Desert ...... 16 5D 29°S 126° E

For places within the British Isles, see British Isles Index on pages 41 - 43

For places within the British Isles, see British Isles Index on pages 41 - 43

For places within the British Isles, see British Isles Index on pages 41 - 43